The Path to Success

Whether you are a new graduate looking for a job or a business owner building a company, *The Art of War* will give you greater insight into achieving success in a competitive world. For over 2,500 years, winners have profited from the ideas of Sun Tzu on how to avoid defeat and embrace victory.

This translation was created out of a desire to create an English version that was completely faithful to the original text. It translator, Gary Gagliardi, is America's leading authority and speaker on using the techniques of *The Art of War* in business. He created this translation after twenty years of studying Sun Tzu and mastering his techniques to build a multimillion dollar business.

The Book is only the beginning...

This book contains **the secret password keys** that allow you to access the Clearbridge Owners' Training Site (see **www.clearbridge.com** for information). This site contains hundred of pages of FREE training material to help you master Sun Tzu's techniques. You can download slide shows, study guides, eBooks, screen savers, posters, and more.

Buy it today and study it forever!

Books for the Art of Business

Other Books from **Clearbridge** Publishing

Amazing Secrets of Sun Tzu's The Art of War
ISBN 1929194072
The Art of War: In Sun Tzu's Own Words
ISBN 1929194005
The Art of War & The Art of Sales
ISBN 1929194013
The Art of War & The Art of Marketing
ISBN 1929194056

The Art of War

In Sun Tzu's Own Words

孫SUN
子TZU
兵WAR
法METHODS

To my wife, Rebecca,
who makes it all wonderful!

THE ART OF WAR

IN SUN TZU'S OWN WORDS

TRANSLATION AND FOREWARD
BY
GARY GAGLIARDI

CLEARBRIDGE PUBLISHING

Published by
Clearbridge Publishing

FIRST EDITION, second printing
Copyright 1999, 2001 © Gary Gagliardi

Manufactured in the United States of America
Front Cover Art by Gary Gagliardi (from 1995 Chinese Republic Stamp)
Back Cover photograph by Davis Freeman

Library of Congress Catalog Card Number: 99-64137
ISBN 1-929194-00-5

Clearbridge Publishing's books may be purchased for business, for any
promotion use or for special sales. Please contact:
Clearbridge PUBLISHING
PO Box 33772, Shoreline, WA 98133
Phone: (206)-533-9357 Fax:(206)-546-9756
www.clearbridge.com
info@clearbridge.com

CONTENTS

FOREWARD IX
PLANNING 3
GOING TO WAR 13
PLANNING AN ATTACK 21
POSITIONING 29
MOMENTUM 37
WEAKNESS AND STRENGTH 45
ARMED CONFLICT 57
ADAPTABILITY 67
ARMED MARCH 73
FIELD POSITION 89
TYPES OF TERRAIN 103
ATTACKING WITH FIRE 125
USING SPIES 133
GLOSSARY OF CHINESE CHARACTERS 142

Foreward

Sun Tzu wrote his famous treatise on war over two thousand years ago. For centuries, the text has been preserved and treasured.

Today, most readers of *The Art of War* are not military men, but business people. They have discovered that Sun Tzu's lessons apply equally well to any struggle for success.

As the first of the military classics, *The Art of War* offers a distinct, non-intuitive philosophy on how to defeat the competition. This philosophy realizes that certain key factors influence the outcome of any confrontation and that victory goes—not to the strongest or most aggressive—but to the person who best understands the true situation

I owe a personal debt of gratitude to the teachings of Sun Tzu. Adapting his principles, we built our software company into a multimillion-dollar business. His teachings strongly influenced our sales and marketing plans. To train our sales people, I wrote a special version called *The Art of Sales*. These ideas helped our company double in size for several years in a row, landing us twice on the Inc. 500 list of fastest growing privately held companies.

When we sold our company, I wanted to bring the wisdom of Sun Tzu to a larger audience. The plan was to offer my adaption of the lessons in *The Art of War* to the sales and marketing battles of the twenty-first century. I had been using the text, from a number of translations, for over twenty years and felt I had developed good insight on Sun Tzu's use in business today.

Originally, I didn't plan to do a new translation of *The Art of War* itself. However, as I delved into the available translations, I discovered that each disagreed on Sun Tzu's meaning at essential points. In order to understand these conflicts, I went back to the Chinese text itself. Even for those who cannot read Chinese, the Internet makes it easy to translate the original Chinese characters. Sites display the Chinese text with links tying each character to different Chinese-English dictionaries. Using the context and other translations to select the appropriate meaning for each character, I created my own character-by-character translation.

After I had translated the characters, I discovered that every English translation embellished some of Sun Tzu's ideas while simultaneously ignoring others. The more I studied Sun Tzu's original words, the less satisfied I was with these translations as the foundation for my other works.

In Sun Tzu, the original Chinese characters are simple and succinct but the ideas that they sketch are rich and complex. In reading his words character-by-character, I developed a deeper appreciation for the text and its layers of meaning.

To share the richness of the text with others, I offer two translations of Sun Tzu. The first is the character-by-character translation I developed in my study of the text. The second is a line-by-line translation of those Chinese phrases into English.

I show these two translations side-by-side. This was important to keep the "weight" of the English identical to the "weight" of original Chinese ideas. Unlike other translations, this version avoids expanding or truncating any part of the text.

This translation also preserves the original context of Sun Tzu's words. In the original text, Sun Tzu grouped the Chinese characters in three ways. The smallest grouping of characters, a Chinese phrase, is a group of from two to ten characters. In the character-by-character translation, a comma or semicolon usually follows these phrases. In the English translation, each Chinese phrase becomes a short English sentence. The next larger grouping of characters is a very long Chinese "sentence" consisting of as many as a dozen phrases. In the English translation, this becomes a number of sentences grouped into a verse, separated by a blank line. The largest grouping is a block of characters consisting of several "sentences." These blocks become a number of verses separated by yin-yang symbols (☯). Each new block begins with a large, bold capital letter.

Through these techniques, we preserve the ideas of Sun Tzu's Chinese in an English translation that comes as close as humanly possible to capturing Sun Tzu's own words. I hope you enjoy his message as much as I have and profit from them at least half as well.

Gary Gagliardi, 1999

Since our original publication of this book in 1999, we have published four other books on Sun Tzu's teaching (see the back of the book for details.) We have also developed a wealth of **FREE on-line materials** *explaining Sun Tzu's concepts in more detail. This information includes hundreds of slides that explain Sun Tzu ideas graphically. It also includes our study guides that examine each verse of the orginal text and our special adaptations. We also have free screen savers, eBooks, poster images and more. You can access this information at* **www.clearbridge.com.**

Gary Gagliardi, 2001

Do you have an company meeting, trade show, or seminar program planned?
Consider a **live presentation** of
THE AMAZING SECRETS OF SUN TZU'S
THE ART OF WAR
By Gary Gagliardi

Contact Clearbridge Publishing
for information.
206-533-9357 info@clearbridge.com

計PLAN 篇Chapter

孫Sun 子Tzu 曰said:
兵War 者thing,
國Nation之's 大big 事profession,
死Death 生birth之's 地ground,
存Life 亡death之's 道philosophy,
不No 可can 不not 察examine 也also.

故Make 經experience 之it 以by 五five 事skills,
校Learn 之it 以by 計planning,
而And yet 索demand 其this 情situation:
一1. 曰Say 道philosophy,
二2. 曰Say 天heaven,
三3. 曰Say 地ground,
四4. 曰Say 將general,
五5. 曰Say 法methods.

道Philosophy 者tthing,
令Command 民people 於from 上above 同similar
意meaning,
可Can 與give 之of 死death,
可Can 與give 之of 生life,
而And yet 不no 畏fear 危danger 詭deceive 也also.

2

Planning

Sun Tzu said:

This is war.
It is the most important skill in the nation.
It is the basis of life and death.
It is the philosophy of survival or destruction.
You must know it well.

Your skill comes from five factors.
Study these factors when you plan war.
You must insist on knowing the nature of:
1. Military philosophy;
2. The weather;
3. The ground;
4. The commander;
5. And military methods.

It starts with your military philosophy.
Command your people in a way that gives them a higher
shared purpose.
You can lead them to death.
You can lead them to life.
They must never fear danger or dishonesty.

天Heaven 者thing,
陰North, shady hillside 陽South, sunny hillside,
寒Cold 暑hot,
時Season 制system 也also.

地Ground 者thing,
遠Distant, 近near,
險Dangerous 易easy,
廣Wide 狹narrow,
死Death 生birth 也also.

將General 者thing,
智Intelligence, 信trust, 仁love, 勇bravery, 嚴strict 也also.

法Method 者thing,
曲Bend 制system,
官Government official 道philosophy,
主Ruler 用use 也also.

凡All 此here 五five 者thing,
將General 莫not 不no 聞hear,
知Knowledge 之of 者thing 勝victory,
不No 知knowledge 之of 者thing 不no 勝victory.

Next, you have the weather.
It can be sunny or overcast.
It can be hot or cold.
It includes the timing of the seasons.

Next is the terrain.
It can be distant or near.
It can be difficult or easy.
It can be open or narrow.
It also determines your life or death.

Next is the commander.
He must be smart, trustworthy, caring, brave and strict.

Finally, you have your military methods.
They include the shape of your organization.
This comes from your management philosophy.
You must master their use.

All five of these factors are critical.
As a commander, you must pay attention to them.
Understanding them brings victory.
Ignoring them means defeat.

故Make 校school 以by 計plans,
而And yet 索demand 其this 情situation.

曰Says:
主Ruler 孰that 有has 道philosophy,
將General 孰that 有has 能ability,
天Weather 地ground 孰that 得obtain,
法Method 令command 孰that 行moves,
兵Army 眾crowd 孰that 強strong,
士Officer 卒soldier 孰that 練train,
賞Reward 罰penalize 孰that 明bright,
吾We 以by 此this 知know 勝victory 負defeat 矣will be;
將General 聽listen 吾our 計plan,
用Uses 之it 必must 勝win,
留Remain 之it;
將General 不no 聽listen 吾our 計plan,
用Uses 之it 必must 負defeat,
去Remove 之it.

計Plan 利advantage 以by means of 聽listening,
乃Therefore 為become 之of 勢power,
以By means of 佐assist 其this 外outside,
勢Situation 者thing,
因Cause 利advantage 而and 制system 權authority 也also.

6

You must learn through planning.
You must question the situation.

You must ask:
Which government has the right philosophy?
Which commander has the skill?
Which season and place has the advantage?
Which method of command works?
Which group of forces has the strength?
Which officers and men have the training?
Which rewards and punishments make sense?
This tells when you will win and when you will lose.
Some commanders perform this analysis.
If you use these commanders, you will win.
Keep them.
Some commanders ignore this analysis.
If you use these commanders, you will lose.
Get rid of them.

Plan an advantage by listening.
This makes you powerful.
Get assistance from the outside.
Know the situation.
Then planning can find opportunities and give you control.

兵War 者thing,
詭Deceive 道philosophy 也also.

故Make 能able 而and yet 示teach 之of 不no 能ability,
用Use 而and yet 示show 不no 用use,
近Near 而and yet 示show 之it 遠far,
遠Distant 而and yet 示show 之it 近near.

利Advantage 而and yet 誘entice 之it,
亂Disorder 而and yet 取choose 之it,
實Substantial 而and yet 備prepare 之it,
強Strong 而and yet 避evade 之it,
怒Rage 而and yet 撓obstruct 之it,
卑Low 而and yet 驕proud 之it,
佚Leisure 而and yet 勞exert 之it,
親Intimate 而and yet 離depart 之it,
攻Attack 其this 無without 備being prepared,
出Exit 其this 不no 意intention.

此Here 兵army 家house 之of 勝victory,
不No 可can 先first 傳pass 也also.

Warfare is one thing.
It is a philosophy of deception.

When you are ready, you try to appear incapacitated.
When active, you pretend inactivity.
When you are close to the enemy, you appear distant.
When far away, pretend you are near.

If the enemy has strong position, entice him away from it.
If the enemy is confused, be decisive.
If the enemy is solid, prepare against him.
If the enemy is strong, avoid him.
If the enemy is angry, frustrate him.
If the enemy is weaker, make him arrogant.
If the enemy is relaxed, make him work.
If the enemy is united, break him apart.
Attack him when he is unprepared.
Leave when he least expects it.

You will find a place where you can win.
Don't pass it by.

夫Husband 未not yet 戰battle 而and yet 廟temple
算counts 勝victory 者thing,
得Obtain 算calculate 多many 也also;
未Not yet 戰battle 而and yet 廟temple 算count 不no
勝victory 者thing,
得Obtain 算calculate 少little 也also;
多Many 算calculates 勝victory,
少Little 算calculate 不no 勝victory,
而And yet 況situation 無without 算calculate 乎??
吾We 以by means of 此this 觀observe 之it,
勝Victory 負defeat 見see 矣will.

Before you go to war, you must believe that you can count on victory.
You must calculate many advantages.
Before you go to battle, you may believe that you can foresee defeat.
You can count few advantages.
Many advantages add up to victory.
Few advantages add up to defeat.
How can you know your advantages without analyzing them?
We can see where we are by means of our observations.
We can foresee our victory or defeat by planning.

作MAKE 戰BATTLE 篇Chapter

孫Sun 子Tzu : 曰said:
凡All 用use 兵war 之's 道philosophy,
馳Speed 車carts 千thousand 駟horse teams,
革Change 車carts 千thousand 乘times,
帶Carry 甲armor 十ten 萬ten thousand,
千Thousand 里miles 饋give 糧grain,
則Then 內internal 外external 之of 費waste,
賓Guest 客visitor之's 用use,
膠Glue 漆lacquer 之of 材lumber,
車Cart 甲armor 之of 奉receive,
曰Say 費waste 千thousand 金metal,
然So 後fall behind 十ten 萬myriad 之of 師troops 舉raise
矣will.

其This 用use 戰battle 也also 貴expensive 勝victory,
久Long time 則then 鈍blunt 兵war 挫defeat 銳sharp,
攻Attack 城city 則then 力power 屈humiliate,
久Long time 暴violent 師troops 則then 國nation 用use
不not 足sufficient.

GOING TO WAR

Sun Tzu said:

Everything depends on your use of military philosophy.
Moving the army requires thousands of vehicles.
These vehicles must be loaded thousands of times.
The army must carry a huge supply of arms.
You need ten thousand acres of grain.
This results in internal and external shortages.
Any army consumes resources like an invader.
It uses up glue and paint for wood.
It requires armor for its vehicles.
People complain about the waste of a vast amount of metal.
It will set you back when you raise tens of thousands of
troops.

Using a huge army makes war very expensive to win.
Long delays create a dull army and sharp defeats.
Attacking enemy cities drains your forces.
Long campaigns that exhaust the nation's resources are
wrong.

夫Husband 鈍blunt 兵war,
挫Defeat 銳sharp,
屈Humiliate 力power,
殫Use up 貨money,
則Then 諸various 侯noblemen 乘multiply by 其this
弊collapse 而and yet 起begin;
雖Although 有have 智intelligence 者one,
不No 能can 善good 其this 後fall behind 矣will be!

故Make 兵war 聞hear 拙careless 速speed,
未Have not 睹seen 巧skillful 之of 久long time 也also.

夫Husband 兵war 久long time 而and yet 國nation
利advantage 者one,
未Have not 之it 有have 也also.

☯

故Because 不no 盡exhaust 知knowledge 用use
兵war之's 害danger 者one,
則Then 不no 能can 盡exhaust 知knowledge 用use
兵war之's 利advantage 也also.

善Good 用use 兵war 者one,
役Military service 不no 再again 籍record,
糧Provisions 不no 三three 載carry,
取Choose 用use 於to 國nation,
因Source 糧provisions 於from 敵enemy,
故Make 軍army 食supplies 可can 足sufficient 也also.

☯

Manage a dull army.
You will suffer sharp defeats.
Drain your forces.
Your money will be used up.
Your rivals multiply as your army collapses and they will
begin against you.
It doesn't matter how smart you are.
You cannot get ahead by taking losses!

You hear of people going to war too quickly.
Still, you won't see a skilled war that lasts a long time.

You can fight a war for a long time or you can make your
nation strong.
You can't do both.

You can never totally understand all the dangers in using
arms.
Therefore, you can never totally understand the advantages
in using arms either.

You want to make good use of war.
Do not raise troops repeatedly.
Do not carry too many supplies.
Choose to be useful to your nation.
Feed off the enemy.
Make your army carry only the provisions it needs.

國Nation 之's 貧poverty 於to 師troops 者thing 遠distant 輸transport,
遠Distant 輸transport 則then 百hundred 姓clans 貧poor,
近Near 于by 師troops 者thing 貴expensive 賣sell,
貴Costly 賣sell 則then 百hundred 姓family 竭exhaust,
財Wealth 竭exhaust 則then 急quickly 於to 丘empty 役military service,
力Force 屈consume 財wealth 殫entirely,
中Among 原former 內internal 虛empty 於from 家households.

百Hundred 姓families 之of 費waste,
十Ten 去go 其this 七seven,
公Public 家households 之of 費waste,
破Broken 軍army 罷dismisses 馬horses,
甲Armor 冑helmet 矢arrow 弩thrown down,
戟Sword 盾shield 蔽conceal 櫓row,
丘Empty 牛ox 大big 車cart,
十Ten 去go 其this 六six.

故Make 智knowledge 將general 務duties 食food 於from 敵enemy.

食Food 敵enemy 一one 鐘cup,
當Equal 吾our 廿twenty 鍾cup,
萁Hay 稈grain 一one 石stone,
當Equal 吾our 廿twenty 石stone.

故Make 殺kill 敵enemy 者ones 怒rage 也also;
取Obtain 敵enemy 之's 利advantage 者thing 貨provisions 也also.

16

The nation impoverishes itself shipping to troops that are far away.
Distant transportation is costly for hundreds of families.
Buying goods with the army nearby is also expensive.
These high prices also impoverish hundreds of families.
People quickly exhaust their resources supporting a military force.
Military forces consume a nation's wealth entirely.
War leaves households in the former heart of the nation with nothing.

War destroys hundreds of families.
Out of every ten families, war leaves only seven.
War empties the government's storehouses.
Broken armies will get rid of their horses.
They will throw down their armor, helmets, and arrows.
They will lose their swords and shields.
They will leave their wagons without oxen.
War will consume sixty percent of everything you have.

Because of this, the commander's duty is to feed off the enemy.

Use a cup of the enemy's food.
It is worth twenty of your own.
Win a bushel of the enemy's feed.
It is worth twenty of your own.

You can kill the enemy and frustrate him as well.
Take the enemy's strength from him by stealing away his supplies.

故Make 車cart 戰battle,
得Obtain 車cart 十ten 乘multiply 以by 上above,
賞Reward 其this 先first 得get 者one,
而And yet 革change 其this 旌banner 旗flag,
車Cart 雜mixed 而and yet 乘multiply 之it,
卒Soldiers 善good 而and yet 養provide for 之it,
是Correct 謂understanding 勝victory 敵enemy 而and yet 益benefit 強strong.

故Make 兵war 貴valuable 勝victory,
不No 貴expensive 久long time,
故Male 知know 兵war 之of 將general,
民People 之of 司government office 命command,
國Nation 家household 安peace 危danger 之of 主ruler 也also.

Fight for the enemy's supply wagons.
Capture their supplies by using overwhelming force.
Reward the first who capture them.
Then change their banners and flags.
Mix them in with your own to increase your supply line.
Keep your soldiers strong by providing for them.
This is what it means to beat the enemy while you grow
more powerful.

Make victory in war pay for itself.
Avoid expensive, long campaigns.
The military commander's knowledge is the key.
It determines if the civilian officials can govern.
It determines if the nation's households are peaceful or a
danger to the state.

謀PLAN 攻ATTACK 篇Chapter

孫Sun 子Tzu 曰said:

凡All 用use 兵war 之's 法methods,
全Complete 國nation 為becomes 上above,
破Broken 國nation 次second-rate 之it,
全Complete 兵war 為becomes 上above,
破Broken 兵war 次second-rate 之it,
全Complete 旅brigade 為becomes 上above,
破Broken 旅brigade 次second-rate 之it,
全Complete 卒men 為becomes 上above,
破Broken 卒men 次second-rate 之it,
全Complete 伍unit 為becomes 上above,
破Broken 伍unit 次second-rate 之it.

是Correct 故make 百hundred 戰battles 百hundred 勝victories,
非Weak 善good 之of 非weak 者thing 也also;
不No 戰battle 而and yet 屈capture 人men 之of 兵war,
善Good 之of 善good 者thing 也also.

20

Planning an Attack

Sun Tzu said:

Everyone relies on the arts of war.
A united nation is strong.
A divided nation is weak.
A united army is strong.
A divided army is weak.
A united force is strong.
A divided force is weak.
United men are strong.
Divided men are weak.
A united unit is strong.
A divided unit is weak.

Unity works because it enables you to win every battle you fight.
Still, this is the foolish goal of a weak leader.
Avoid battle and make the enemy's men surrender.
This is the right goal for a superior leader.

故Make 上above 兵war 伐cutdown 謀scheme,
其This 次second-rate 伐cutdown 交meet,
其This 次second-rate 伐cutdown 兵war,
其This 下below 攻attack 城city.

攻Attack 城city 之of 法method,
為Become 不no 得obtain 已stop;
修Fix 櫓row 轒chariot 轀hearse,
其This 器equipment 械machinery,
三Three 用use 而and yet 後fall behind 成accomplish,
距Distance 闉enclose,
又Again 三three 用use 而and yet 後fall behind 已stop;
將General 不no 勝victory 其this 忿anger,
而And yet 蟻insect 附add to 之it,
殺Kill 士officers 卒men 三three 分separate 之of 一one,
而And yet 城city 不no 拔pull out 者one,
此Here 攻attack 之of 災disaster 也also.

故Make 善good 用use 兵war 者one,
屈Surrender 人people 之's 兵war;
而And yet 非weak 戰battle 也also;
拔Pull out 人men 之of 城city,
而And yet 非weak 攻attack 也also;
毀Destroy 人men 之of 國nation,
而And yet 非weak 久long time 也also.

The best policy is to attack while the enemy is still planning.
The next best is to disrupt alliances.
The next best is to attack the opposing army.
The worst is to attack the enemy's cities.

This is what happens when you attack a city.
You can attempt it, but you can't finish it.
First you must make siege engines.
You need the right equipment and machinery.
You use three months and still cannot win.
Then, you try to encircle the area.
You use three more months without making progress.
The commander still doesn't win and this angers him.
He then tries to swarm the city.
This kills a third of his officers and men.
He still isn't able to draw the enemy out of the city.
This attack is a disaster.

Make good use of war.
Make the enemy's troops surrender.
You can do this fighting only minor battles.
You can draw their men out of their cities.
You can do it with small attacks.
You can destroy the men of a nation.
You must keep your campaign short.

必Must 以by 全complete 爭conflict 於to 天heaven 下below,
故Make 兵war 不no 頓pause,
利Advantage 可can 全complete,
此Here 謀plan 攻attack 之of 法method 也also.

故Make 用use 兵war 之's 法method,
十Ten 則then 圍encircle 之it,
五Five 則then 攻attack 之it,
倍Times 則then 分divide 之it,
敵Enemy 則then 能can 戰battle 之it,
少Small 則then 能can 守defend 之it,
不No 若like 則then 能can 避evade 之it.

故Make 少small 敵enemy 之of 堅firm,
大Big 故enemy 之of 擒catch 也also.

☯

夫Husband 將general 者one,
國Nation 之's 輔assist 也also.

輔Assist 周helps 則then 國nation 必must 強powerful,
輔Assist 隙split 則then 國nation 必must 弱weak.

故Make 軍army 之's 所place 以by 患problem 於from 君lord
者one 三three:
不No 知know 三three 軍army 之's 不no 可can 以by
進advance 而and yet 謂call 進advance,
不No 知know 三three 軍army 之's 不no 可can 以by means
of 退withdrawn 而and yet 謂call 退withdraw,
是Correct 謂call 縻tie up 軍army;
不No 知know 三three 軍army 之's 事profession,
而And yet 同same 三three 軍army 之's 任govern,
則Then 軍army 士officers 惑confused 矣will be.

24

You must use total war, fighting with everything you have.
Never stop fighting when at war.
You can gain complete advantage.
To do this, you must plan your strategy of attack.

The rules for making war are:
If you outnumber the enemy ten to one, surround them.
If you outnumber them five to one, attack them.
If you outnumber them two to one, divide them.
If you are equal, then find an advantageous battle.
If you are fewer, defend against them.
If you are much weaker, evade them.

Small forces are not powerful.
However, large forces cannot catch them.

You must master command.
The nation must support you.

Supporting the military makes the nation powerful.
Not supporting the military makes the nation weak.

Politicians create problems for the military in three different
ways.
Ignorant of the army's inability to advance, they order an
advance.
Ignorant of the army's inability to withdraw, they order a
withdrawal.
We call this tying up the army.
Politicians don't understand the army's business.
Still, they think they can run an army.
This confuses the army's officers.

不No 知knowledge 三three 軍armies 之's 權authority,
而And yet 同same 三three 軍armies 之's 任permission,
則Then 軍army 士officers 疑doubtful 矣will be.

三Three 軍army 既both 惑confused 且and 疑doubtful,
則Then 諸various 侯noblemen 之's 難disaster 至arrive 矣will,
是Correct 謂call 亂disorder 軍army 引pull 勝victory.

故Make 知know 勝victory 有have 五five:
知Knowledge 可can 以by mean of 戰battle 與give 不no
可can 以by means of 戰battle 者one 勝victory,
識Knowledge 眾crowd 寡scarce 之of 用use 者one
勝victory,
上Above 下below 同same 欲desire 者one 勝victory,
以By 虞worry 得obtain 不no 虞worry 者one 勝victory,
將General 能able 而and yet 君monarch 不no 御drive 者one
勝victory,
此Here 五five 者things,
知Know 勝victory 之's 道philosophy 也also.

故Make 曰said:
知Know 彼each other 知know 己self,
百Hundred 戰battles 不no 殆dangerous,
不No 知know 彼each other 而and yet 知know 己self,
一One 勝victory 一one 負defeat,
不No 知know 彼each other 不no 知know 己self,
每Every 戰battle 必must 敗defeat.

Politicians don't know the army's chain of command.
They give the army too much freedom.
This will create distrust among the army's officers.

The entire army becomes confused and distrusting.
This invites the invasion from many different rivals.
We say correctly that disorder in an army kills victory.

You must know five things to win:
Victory comes from knowing when to attack and when to avoid battle.
Victory comes from correctly using both large and small forces.
Victory comes from everyone sharing the same goals.
Victory comes from finding opportunities in problems.
Victory comes from having a capable commander and the government leaving him alone.
You must know these five things.
You then know the theory of victory.

We say:
"Know yourself and know your enemy.
You will be safe in every battle.
You may know yourself but not know the enemy.
You will then lose one battle for every one you win.
You may not know yourself or the enemy.
You will then lose every battle."

形FORM 篇Chapter

孫Sun 子Tzu 曰said:
昔Ancient 之of 善good 戰battle 者one,
先First 為become 不no 可able 勝win,
以By means of 侍serve 敵enemy 之it 可able 勝win,
不No 可able 勝win 在exist 己self,
可Able 勝win 在exist 敵enemy.

故Make 善good 戰battle 者one,
能Can 為become 不no 可able 勝victory,
不No 能can 使use敵enemy 必must 可able 勝victory.

故Make 曰say:
勝Victory 可can 知know 而and yet 不no 可can 為become.

不No 可can 勝victory 者one,
守Defend 也also;
可Can 勝victory 者one,
攻Attack 也bvalso,
守Defend 則then 不no 足sufficient,
攻Attack 則then 則has 餘excess.

28

POSITIONING

Sun Tzu said:

Learn from the history of successful battles.
Your first actions should deny victory to the enemy.
You pay attention to your enemy to find the way to win.
You alone can deny victory to the enemy.
Only your enemy can allow you to win.

You must fight well.
You can prevent the enemy's victory.
You cannot win unless the enemy enables your victory.

We say:
You see the opportunity for victory; you don't create it.

You are sometimes unable to win.
You must then defend.
You will eventually be able to win.
You must then attack.
Defend when you have insufficient strength to win.
Attack when you have more strength than you need to win.

善Good 守defend 者one,
藏Save 於from 九nine 此place 之of 下below,
善Good 攻attack 者one,
動Move 於to 九nine 天heaven 之of 上above.

故Make 能can 自self 保preserve 而and yet 全complete
勝victory 也also.

見See 勝victory,
不No 過pass 眾crowd 人men 之's 所place 知know,
非Weak 善good 之of 善good 者one 也also.

戰Battle 勝victory 而and yet 天heaven 下below 曰say
善good,
非Weak 善good 之of 善good 者one 也also.

故Make 舉raise 秋autumn 毫thousandth,
不No 為become 多many 力force;
見See 日day 用use,
不No 為become 明bright 目eye,
聞Hear 雷thunder 霆clap,
不No 為become 聰clever 耳ear.

古Ancient 之of 善good 戰battle 者one,
勝Victory 於to 易easy 勝victory 者one 也also;
故Make 善good 戰battle 者one 之of 勝victory 也also,
無Without 智intelligence 名name,
無Without 勇bravery 功accomplishment.

You must defend yourself well.
Save your forces and dig in.
You must attack well.
Move your forces when you have a clear advantage.

You must protect your forces until you can completely
triumph.

Some may see how to win.
However, they cannot position their forces where they must.
This demonstrates limited ability.

Some can struggle to a victory and the whole world may
praise their winning.
This also demonstrates a limited ability.

Win as easily as picking up a fallen hair.
Don't use all of your forces.
See the time to move.
Don't try to find something clever.
Hear the clap of thunder.
Don't try to hear something subtle.

Learn from the history of successful battles.
Victory goes to those who make winning easy.
A good battle is one that you will obviously win.
It doesn't take intelligence to win a reputation.
It doesn't take courage to achieve success.

故Make 其this 戰battle 勝victory 不no 忒excess,
不No 忒excess 者one,
其This 措position 必must 勝win,
勝Victory 已stop 敗defeat 者one 也also.

故Make 善good 戰battle 者one,
立Stand 於to 不no 敗defeat 之of 地place,
而And yet 不no 失lose 敵enemy之's 敗defeat 也also.

是Correct 故make 勝victory 兵war 先first 勝victory,
而And yet 後afterward 求strive for 戰battle,
敗Defeat 兵war 先first 戰battle 而and yet 後afterwards
求strive for 勝victory.

☯

善Good 用use 兵war 者one,
修Study 道philosophy 而and yet 保preserve 法method,
故Make 能can 為become 勝victory 敗defeat之's 政ruler.

兵War 法methods:
"一1. 曰Say 度measure,
二2. 曰Say 量quantity,
三3. 曰Say 數count,
四4. 曰Say 稱weigh,
五5. 曰Say 勝victory,
地Place 生birth 度measure,
度Measure 生birth 量quantity,
量Quantity 生birth 數count,
數Count 生birth 稱weigh,
稱Weigh 生birth 勝victory."

You must win your battles without effort.
Avoid difficult struggles.
Fight when your position must win.
You always win by preventing your defeat.

You must engage only in winning battles.
Position yourself where you cannot lose.
Never waste an opportunity to defeat your enemy.

You win a war by first assuring yourself of victory.
Only afterward do you look for a fight.
Outmaneuver the enemy before the battle and then fight to win.

You must make good use of war.
Study military philosophy and the art of defense.
You can control your victory or defeat.

This is the art of war.
"1. Discuss the distances.
  2. Discuss your numbers.
  3. Discuss your calculations.
  4. Discuss your decisions.
  5. Discuss victory.
The ground determines the distance.
The distance determines your numbers.
Your numbers determine your calculations.
Your calculations determine your decisions.
Your decisions determine your victory."

故Make 勝victory 兵war 若seem 以by means of
鎰amount of gold 稱weigh 銖amount of silver,
敗Defeat 兵war 若seem 以by means of 銖amount of silver
稱weigh 鎰amount of gold.

勝Victory 者thing 之of 戰battle 民people 也also,
若Seem 決wash 積accumulate 水water 於through
千thousand 仞fathom 之of 谿gorge 者thing,
形Form 也also.

34

Creating a winning war is like balancing a coin of gold against
a coin of silver.
Creating a losing war is like balancing a coin of silver against
a coin of gold.

Winning a battle is always a matter of people.
You pour them into battle like a flood of water pouring into
a deep gorge.
This is a matter of positioning.

勢FORCE 篇Chapter

孫Sun 子Tzu 曰said:

凡All 治control 眾crowd 如as if 治control 寡few,
分Separate 數number 是correct 也also;
鬥Fight 眾crowd 如as if 鬥fight 寡few,
形Forms 名names 是correctly 也also;
三Three 軍army 之of 眾crowd,
可May 使make 必must 受receive 敵enemy 而and yet
無without 敗defeat 者one,
奇Unusual 正straight 是correct 也also;
兵War 之's 所place 加increase,
如As if 以by means of 碬order 投throw 卵eggs 者one,
虛Insubstantial 實Substantial 是correct 也also.

凡All 戰battle 者one,
以By means of 正straight 合join,
以By means of 奇unusual 勝win.

故Make 善good 出exit 奇unusual 者one,
無Without 窮limit 如as if 天heaven 所place,
不No 竭exhaust 如as if 江river 河stream.

MOMENTUM

Sun Tzu said:

You control a large group the same as you control a few.
You just divide their ranks correctly.
You fight a large army the same as you fight a small one.
You only need the right position and communication.
You may meet a large enemy army.
You must be able to encounter the enemy without being defeated.
You must correctly use both surprise and direct action.
Your army's position must increase your strength.
Troops flanking an enemy can smash them like eggs.
You must correctly use both strength and weakness.

It is the same in all battles.
You use a direct approach to engage the enemy.
You use surprise to win.

You must use surprise for a successful invasion.
Surprise is as infinite as the weather and land.
Surprise is as inexhaustible as the flow of a river.

終End 而and yet 復return to 始start,
日Day 月month 是correct 也also.

死Dead 而and yet 復return to 復birth,
四Four 時season 是correct 也also.

聲Tone 不no 過pass 五five,
五Five 聲tone 之's 變change,
不No 可can 勝victory 聽listen 也also.

色Color 不no 過pass 五five,
五Five 色color 之's 變change,
不No 可can 勝victory 觀observe 也also.

味Smell 不no 過pass 五five,
五Five 味smell 之of 變change,
不No 可can 勝victory 嘗taste 也also.

戰Battle 勢force,
不No 過pass 奇unusual 正straight,
奇Unusual 正straight 之's 變change,
不No 可can 勝victory 窮limit 也also.

奇Unusual 正straight 相mutually 生born,
如As if 循proceed 環circle 之's 無without 端end,
孰Which 能can 窮limit 之it 哉alas!

You can be stopped and yet recover the initiative.
You must use your days and months correctly.

If you are defeated, you can recover.
You must use the four seasons correctly.

There are only a few notes in the scale.
Yet, you can always rearrange them.
You can never hear every song of victory.

There are only a few basic colors.
Yet, you can always mix them.
You can never see all the shades of victory.

There are only a few flavors.
Yet, you can always blend them.
You can never taste all the flavors of victory.

You fight with momentum.
There are only a few types of surprises and direct actions.
Yet, you can always vary the ones you use.
There is no limit in the ways you can win.

Surprise and direct action give birth to each other.
They proceed from each other in an endless cycle.
You can not exhaust all their possible combinations!

☯

激Flow 水water 之of 疾rapid,
至Stop 於to 漂float 石rock 者one,
勢Force 也also.

鷙Hawk 鳥bird 之of 擊strike,
至Stop 於to 毀destroy 折suffer loss 者one,
節Restrain 也also.

是Correct 故make 善good 戰battle 者one,
其This 勢force 險dangerous,
其This 節restrain 短brief.

勢Force 如comparable to 張stretch 弩crossbow,
節Restrain 如comparable to 機machine 發shoot.

紛Confused 紛confused 紜tangled 紜tangled,
鬥Fight 亂disorder,
而And yet 不no 可may 亂disorder 也also.

渾Muddy 渾muddy 沌murky 沌murky,
形Form 圓round,
而And yet 不no 可may 敗defeat 也also.

亂Disorder 生birth 於to 治rule,
怯Fear 生birth 於to 勇bravery,
弱Weak 生birth 於to 強strong.

治Rule 亂disorder,
數Number 也also;
勇Brave 怯fear,
勢Force 也also.

Surging water flows together rapidly.
Its pressure washes away boulders.
This is momentum.

A hawk suddenly strikes a bird.
Its contact alone kills the prey.
This is timing.

You must fight only winning battles.
Your momentum must be overwhelming.
Your timing must be exact.

Your momentum is like the tension of a bent crossbow.
Your timing is like the pulling of a trigger.

War is very complicated and confused.
Battle is chaotic.
Nevertheless, you must not allow chaos.

War is very sloppy and messy.
Positions turn around.
Nevertheless, you must never be defeated.

Chaos gives birth to control.
Fear gives birth to courage.
Weakness gives birth to strength.

You must control chaos.
This depends on your planning.
Your men must brave their fears.
This depends on their momentum.

強Strength 弱weakness,
形Form 也also.

故Make 善good 動move 敵enemy 者one,
形Form 之it,
敵Enemy 必must 從follow 之it;
予Give 之it,
敵Enemy 必must 取take 之it,
以By means of 利advantage 動move 之it,
以By means of 卒soldiers 動move 之it,
以By means of 實substantial 待stay 之it.

故Make 善good 戰battle 者one,
求Seek 之it 於from 勢force,
不No 責demand 於from 人men,
故Make 能able 擇choose 人men 而and 任allow 勢force.

任Allow 勢force 者one,
其This 戰battle 人men 也also,
如Compare to 轉roll 木trees 石stones,
木Tree 石stones 之of 性nature,
安Console 則then 靜tranquil,
危Danger 則then 動move,
方Direction 則then 止stop,
圓Round 則then 行march.

故Make 善good 戰battle 者men 之's 勢force,
如As if 轉roll 圓round 石rocks 於to 千thousand
仞fathoms 之's 上above 者one,
勢Force 也also.

You have strengths and weaknesses.
These come from your position.

You must force the enemy to move to your advantage.
Use your position.
The enemy must follow you.
Surrender a position.
The enemy must take it.
You can offer an advantage to move him.
You can use your men to move him.
You use your strength to hold him.

You want a successful battle.
To do this, you must seek momentum.
Do not just demand a good fight from your people.
You must pick good people and then give them momentum.

You must create momentum.
You create it with your men during battle.
This is comparable to rolling trees and stones.
Trees and stones roll because of their shape and weight.
Offer men safety and they will stay calm.
Endanger them and they will act.
Give them a place and they will hold.
Round them up and they will march.

You make your men powerful in battle with momentum.
This is just like rolling round stones down over a high, steep cliff.
Use your momentum.

虚EMPTY 實FULL 篇Chapter

孫Sun 子Tzu 曰said:
凡All 先first 虚empty 戰battle 地 ground 而and yet 待wait
敵enemy 者one 佚leisure,
後After 虚empty 戰battle 地ground 而and yet 趨hurry
戰battle 者one 勞exert.

故Make 善good 戰battle 者one,
致Send 人men 而and yet 不not 致send 於to 人men.

能Can 使cause 敵enemy 自self 至arrive 者one,
利Benefit 之it 也also;
能Can 使cause 敵enemy 不not 得gain 至arrive 者one,
害Misfortune 之it 也also.

故Make 敵enemy 佚relaxed 能can 勞weary 之it,
飽Satisfied 能can 飢starve 之it,
安Peaceful 能can 動move 之it.

44

Weakness and Strength

Sun Tzu said:

Always arrive first to the empty battlefield to await the enemy at your leisure.
If you are late and hurry to the battlefield, fighting is more difficult.

You want a successful battle.
Move your men, but not into opposing forces.

You can make the enemy come to you.
Offer him an advantage.
You can make the enemy avoid coming to you.
Threaten him with danger.

When the enemy is fresh, you can tire him.
When he is well fed, you can starve him.
When he is relaxed, you can move him.

出Exit 其this 所place 不no 趨hurry,
趨Hurry 其this 所place 不no 意intention;
行March 千thousand 里miles 而but 不no 勞weary 者one,
行March 於to 無without 人man 之go 地place 也also;
攻Attack 而and yet 必must 取take 者one,
攻Attack 其this 所place 不no 守defend 也also;
守Defend 而but 必must 固walls 者one,
守Defend 其this 所place 不no 攻attack 也also.

故Make 善good 攻attack 者one,
敵Enemy 不no 知knowledge 其this 所place 守defend.

善Good 守defense 者one,
敵Enemy 不no 知knowledge 其this 所place 攻attack.

微Tiny乎! 微Tiny乎!
至Arrive 於to 無without 形form;
神Spirit乎! 神Spirit乎!
至Arrive 於to 無without 聲sound,
故Make 能can 為become 敵enemy之's 司manage 命destiny.

進Advance 而but 不no 可can 禦defend 者one,
衝Charge 其this 虛empty 也also;
退Withdraw 而but 不no 可can 追chase 者one,
速Rapid 而but 不no 可can 及reach 也also

46

Leave any place without haste.
Hurry to where you are unexpected.
You can easily march hundreds of miles without tiring.
To do so, travel through areas that are deserted.
You must take whatever you attack.
Attack when there is no defense.
You must have walls to defend.
Defend where it is impossible to attack.

Be skilled in attacking.
Give the enemy no idea of where to defend.

Be skillful in your defense.
Give the enemy no idea of where to attack.

Be subtle! Be subtle!
Arrive without any clear formation.
Quietly! Quietly!
Arrive without a sound.
You must use all your skill to control the enemy's decisions.

Advance where they can't defend.
Charge through their openings.
Withdraw where the enemy cannot chase you.
Move quickly so that they cannot catch you.

故Make 我I 欲desire 戰battle,
敵Enemy 雖although 高high 壘rampart 深deep 溝moat,
不No 得obtain 不no 與give 我I 戰battle 者one,
攻Attack 其this 所place 必must 救rescue 也also;
我I 不no 欲desire 戰battle,
劃Divide 地ground 而and yet 守defend 之it,
敵Enemy 不no 得need 與give 我I 戰battle 者one,
乖Oppose 其this 所place 之go 也also.

故Make 形form 人men 而but 我I 無without 形form,
則Then 我I 專concentrate 而but 敵enemy 分separate;
我I 專concentrate 為become 一one,
敵Enemy 分divide 為become 十ten,
是Correct 以by mean of 十ten 攻attack 其this 一one 也also;
則Then 我I 眾crowd 而but 敵enemy 寡few,
能Can 以by-means of 眾crowd 擊strike 寡few,
則Then 我I 之go 所place 與give 敵enemy 者one,
約Schedule 矣will.

吾Our 所place 與give 戰battle之's 地ground 不no 可can
知know,
不No 可can 知know,
則Then 敵enemy 所place 備prepared 者thing 多many,
敵Enemy 所place 備prepared 者thing 多many,
則Then 我my 所place 與give 戰battle 者thing,
寡Scarce 矣will be.

I always pick my own battles.
The enemy can hide behind high walls and deep trenches.
I do not try to win by fighting him directly.
Instead, I attack a place that he must rescue.
I avoid the battles that I don't want.
I can divide the ground and yet defend it.
I don't give the enemy anything to win.
Divert him from coming to where you defend.

I make their men take a position while I take none.
I then focus my forces where the enemy divides his forces.
Where I focus, I unite my forces.
When the enemy divides, he creates many small groups.
I want my large group to attack one of his small ones.
Then I have many men where the enemy has but a few.
My large force can overwhelm his small one.
I then go on to the next small enemy group.
I will take them one at a time.

We must keep the place that we've chosen as a battleground
a secret.
The enemy must not know.
Force the enemy to prepare his defense in many places.
I want the enemy to defend many places.
Then I can choose where to fight.
His forces will be weak there.

故Make 備prepared 前front 則then 後behind 寡scarce,
備Prepare 後behind 前then 前front 寡scarce,
備Prepare 左left 前then 右right 寡scarce,
備Prepare 右right 前then 左left 寡scarce,
無Without 所place 不no 備prepare,
則Then 無without 所place 不no 寡scarce.

寡Scarce 者one,
備Prepare 人men 者one 也also;
眾Crowd 者one,
使Make 人men 備prepare 己self 者one 也also.

故Make 知knowledge 戰battle 之's 地ground,
知Know 戰battle 之's 日day,
則Then 可can 千thousand 里miles 而but 會make 戰battle.

不No 知know 戰battle 之's 地place,
不No 知know 戰battle 之's 日day,
則Then 左left 不no 能can 救rescue 右right,
右Right 不no 能can 救rescue 左left,
前Front 不no 能can 救rescue 後back,
後Back 不no 能can 救rescue 前front,
而But 況situation 遠distant 者one 數number 十ten 里miles,
近Near 者one 數count 里miles 乎what?

以By means of 吾our 度measure 之it,
越Excess 人men 之of 兵war 雖although 多many,
亦Also 奚why 益augment 於to 勝victory 哉alas?

50

If he reinforces his front lines, he depletes his rear.
If he reinforces his rear, he depletes his front.
If he reinforces his right flank, he depletes his left.
If he reinforces his left flank, he depletes his right.
Without knowing the place of attack, he cannot prepare.
Without knowing the right place, he will be weak everywhere.

The enemy has weak points.
Prepare your men against them.
He has strong points.
Make his men prepare themselves against you.

You must know the battle ground.
You must know the time of battle.
You can then travel a thousand miles and still win the battle.

The enemy should not know the battleground.
He shouldn't know the time of battle.
His left will be unable to support his right.
His right will be unable to support his left.
His front lines will be unable to support his rear.
His rear will be unable to support his front.
His support is distant even if it is only ten miles away.
What unknown place can be close?

We control the balance of forces.
The enemy may have many men but they are superfluous.
How can they help him to victory?

哉It's 曰said:
勝Victory 可can 為become 也also.

敵Enemy 雖although 眾crowd,
可Can 使use 無without 鬥fight.

故Make 策strategy 之it 而and yet 知know 得gain 失loss 之of 計plan,
作Use 之it 而and yet 其know 動action 靜non-action 之's 理administration,
形Form 之it 而and yet 知know 死death 生birth 之of 地ground,
角Contend 之it 而and yet 知know 有have 餘excess 不not 足sufficient 之of 處management.

故Make 形form 兵war 之's 極ridgepole,
至Arrive 於to 無without 形form,
無Without 形form,
則Then 深deep 間spies 不no 能can 窺spy on,
智Wise 者one 不no 能can 謀plan;
因Follow 形form 而and yet 措arrange 勝victory 於to 眾crowd,
眾Crowd 不no 能can 知know,
人Men 皆together 知know 我my 所place 以by means of 勝victory 之's 形form,
而And yet 其not 知know 吾our 所place 以by means of 制control 勝victory 之's 形form;
故Make 其this 戰battle 勝victory 不no 復recover,
而And yet 應comply with 形form 無without 窮limit.

We say:
You must let victory happen.

The enemy may have many men.
You can still control him without a fight.

When you form your strategy, know the strengths and
weaknesses of your plan.
When you execute, know how to manage both action and
inaction.
When you take a position, know the deadly and the winning
grounds.
When you battle, know when you have too many or too few
men.

Use your position as your war's centerpiece.
Arrive at the battle without a formation.
Don't take a position.
Then even the best spies can't report it.
Even the wisest general cannot plan to counter you.
Take a position where you can triumph using superior
numbers.
Keep the enemy's forces ignorant.
Their troops will learn of my location when my position will
win.
They must not know how our location gives us a winning
position.
Make the battle one from which they cannot recover.
You must always adjust your position to their position.

夫Husband 兵war 形form 象image 水water,
水Water 之goes 形form,
避Avoid 高high 而and yet 趨tend toward 下low;
兵War 之goes 形form,
避Avoid 實full 而and yet 擊strike 虛empty;
水Water 因follows 地earth and yet 制control 流flow,
兵War 因follows 敵enemy 而and yet 制controls 勝victory.

故Make 兵war 無without 常ruler 勢influence,
水Water 無without 常ruler 形form;
能Can 因follow 敵enemy 變transform 化change 而and yet
取obtain 勝victory,
謂Name 之's 神spirit.

故Make 五five 行march 無without 常ruler 勝victory,
四Four 時seasons 無without 常ruler 位position,
日Day 有has 短brief 長length,
月Month 有has 死death 生birth.

Manage your military position like water.
Water takes every shape.
It avoids the high and moves to the low.
Your war can take any shape.
It must avoid the strong and strike the weak.
Water follows the shape of the land that directs its flow.
Your forces follow the enemy who determines how you win.

Make war without a standard approach.
Water has no consistent shape.
If you follow the enemy's shifts and changes, you can always
win.
We call this shadowing.

Fight five different campaigns without a firm rule for victory.
Use all four seasons without a consistent position.
Your timing must be sudden.
A few weeks determine your failure or success.

軍ARMY 爭CONFLICT 篇Chapter

孫Sun 子Tzu 曰said:
凡All 用use 兵war之's 法methods,
將General 受endure 命order 於to 君monarch,
合Join 軍armed 聚masses 眾crowd,
交Meet 和harmoniously 而and yet 舍shelter,
莫Not 難disaster 於through 軍armed 爭conflict.

軍Armed 爭conflict 之of 難disaster 者one,
以By means of 迂detour 為become 直direct,
以By means of 患problem 為become 利advantage.

故Make 迂detour 其this 途roadway,
而And yet 誘guide 之it 以by means of 利advantage,
後Behind 人men 發shoot,
先Front 人men 至arrive,
此Here 知know 迂detour 直straight 之of 計plan 者thing
也also.

故Make 軍armed 爭conflict 為become 利advantage,
軍Armed 爭conflict 為become 危danger.

ARMED CONFLICT

Sun Tzu said:

Everyone uses the arts of war.
You accept orders from the government.
Then you assemble your army.
You organize your men and build camps.
You must avoid disasters from armed conflict.

Seeking armed conflict can be disastrous.
Because of this, a detour can be the shortest path.
Because of this, problems can become opportunities.

Use an indirect route as your highway.
Use the search for advantage to guide you.
When you fall behind, you must catch up.
When you get ahead, you must wait.
You must know the detour that most directly accomplishes
your plan.

Undertake armed conflict when you have an advantage.
Seeking armed conflict for its own sake is dangerous.

☯

舉Raise 軍army 而and yet 爭conflict 利advantage,
則Then 不no 及reach;
委Entrust 軍army 而and yet 爭conflict 利advantage,
則Then 輜wagon 重heavy 捐discard.

是Straight 故make 卷roll 甲armor 而and yet 趨hurry,
日Day 夜night 不no 處manage,
倍Multiple 道way 兼unite 行march,
百Hundred 里miles 而and yet 爭conflict 利advantage,
則Then 擒catch 三three 將general 軍army,
勁Powerful 者one 先first,
疲Weak 者one 後follows,
其This 法method 十ten 一one 而and yet 至arrive;
五Five 十ten 里miles 而and yet 爭conflict 利advantage,
則Then 蹶trip 上up 將general 軍army,
其This 法method 半half 至arrive,
卅Thirty 里miles 而yet 爭conflict 利advantage,
則Then 三three 分divide 之of 二two 至arrive.

是Correct 故cause 軍army 無without 輜wagon 重heavy 則then 亡die,
無Without 糧provisions 食food 則then 亡die,
無Without 委yield 積save 則then 亡die.

You can build up an army to fight for an advantage.
Then you won't catch the enemy.
You can force your army to go fight for an advantage.
Then you abandon your heavy supply wagons.

You keep only your armor and hurry after the enemy.
You avoid stopping day or night.
You use many roads at the same time.
You go hundreds of miles to fight for an advantage.
Then the enemy catches your commanders and your army.
Your strong soldiers get there first.
Your weaker soldiers follow behind.
Using this approach, only one in ten will arrive.
You can try to go fifty miles to fight for an advantage.
Then your commanders and army will stumble.
Using this method, only half of your soldiers will make it.
You can try to go thirty miles to fight for an advantage.
Then only two out of three get there.

If you make your army travel without good supply lines, they
will die.
Without supplies and food, your army will die.
If you don't save the harvest, your army will die.

故Make 不no 知know 諸various 侯noblemen 之of 謀plan
者thing,
不No 能can 豫hesitate 交meet;
不No 知know 山mountain 林forest,
險Obstruction 阻block,
沮Prevention 澤pond 之of 形form 者thing,
不No 能can 行march 軍army;
不No 用use 嚮towards 導guide 者thing,
不No 能can 得obtain 地ground 利advantage.

☯

故Make 兵war 以by means of 詐deceive 立stand,
以By this means 則then 動act,
以By this means 分divide 和harmony 為become
變transform 者thing 也also,
故Make 其this 疾swift 如like 風wind,
其This 餘great 如like 林forest,
侵Invade 掠plunder 如like 火fire,
不No 動act 如like 山mountain,
難Disaster 知knowledge 如like 陰clouds,
動Act 如like 雷thunder 霆clap.

掠Plunder 鄉hometown 分divide 眾many,
廓Boundless 地ground 分divide 利advantage,
懸Suspend 權authority 而and yet 動act,
先First 知know 迂detour 直straight 之of 計plan 者one
勝victory,
此Here 軍army 爭conflict 之of 法method 也also.

☯

60

Do not let any of your potential enemies know of what you are planning.
Still, you must not hesitate to form alliances.
You must know the mountains and forests.
You must know where the obstructions are.
You must know where the marshes are.
If you don't, you cannot move the army.
If you don't, you must use local guides.
If you don't, you can't take advantage of the terrain.

You make war using a deceptive position.
If you use deception, then you can move.
Using deception, you can upset the enemy and change the situation.
You can move as quickly as the wind.
You can rise like the forest.
You can invade and plunder like fire.
You can stay as motionless as a mountain.
You can be as mysterious as the fog.
You can strike like sounding thunder.

Divide your troops to plunder the villages.
When on open ground, dividing is an advantage.
Don't worry about organization, just move.
Be the first to find a new route that leads directly to a winning plan.
This is the how you are successful at armed conflict.

軍Army 政correctness 曰says:
"言Speak 不not 相examine 聞hear,
故Make 為become 金metal 鼓drum;
視See 不not 相examine 見view,
故Make 為become 旌banner 旗flags."

夫Husband 金metal 鼓drum 旌banner 旗flag 者one,
所Place 以by means of 一one 人man 之's 耳ear 目eye 也also;
人Man 既both 專concentrate 者one,
則Then 勇brave 者one 不not 得get 獨alone 進advance,
怯Cowardly 者one 不not 得get 獨alone 退retreat,
此This 用use 眾crowd 之's 法method 也also.

故Make 夜night 戰battle 多many 火fires 鼓drums,
晝Daytime 戰battle 多many 旌banners 旗flags,
所Place 以by means of 變change 人man 之's 耳ear 目eye
也also.

故Make 三three 軍armies 可can 奪seize 氣spirit,
將General 軍army 可can 奪seize 心feeling.

是Correct 故cause 朝morning 氣spirit 銳sharp,
晝Daytime 氣spirit 惰lazy,
暮Dusk 氣spirit 歸return home;
故Make 善good 用use 兵war 者one,
避Avoid 其this 銳sharp 氣spirit,
擊Strike 其this 惰lazy 歸return home,
此Here 治govern 氣spirit 者one 也also.

Military experience says:
"You can speak, but you will not be heard.
You must use gongs and drums.
You cannot really see your forces just by looking.
You must use banners and flags."

You must master gongs, drums, banners and flags.
Place people as a single unit where they can all see and hear.
You must unite them as one.
Then, the brave cannot advance alone.
The fearful cannot withdraw alone.
You must force them to act as a group.

In night battles, you must use numerous fires and drums.
In day battles, you must use many banners and flags.
You must position your people to control what they see and hear.

You control your army by controlling its emotions.
As a general, you must be able to control emotions.

In the morning, a person's energy is high.
During the day, it fades.
By evening, a person's thoughts turn to home.
You must use your troops wisely.
Avoid the enemy's high spirits.
Strike when they are lazy and want to go home.
This is how you master energy.

以By means of 治govern 待await 亂disorder,
以By means of 靜tranquil 待await 譁uproar,
此Here 治govern 心feelings 者one 也also.

以By means of 近near 待await 遠distant,
以By means of 佚leisure 待await 勞weary,
以By means of 飽satisfaction 待await 飢starving,
此Here 治govern 力power 者one 也also.

無Without 邀invitation 正right 正correct之's 旗banner,
勿Do not 擊attack 堂hall 堂hall 之of 陣formation,
此Here 治govern 變transform 者one 也also;
故Make 用use 兵war之's 法method,
高High 陵mound 勿do not 向face,
背Back 邱walls 勿do not 逆oppose,
佯Pretend 北flee 勿do not 從follow,
銳Sharp 卒soldiers 勿do not 攻attack,
餌Bait 兵war 勿do not 食feed,
歸Returning home 師troops 勿do not 遏block,
圍Encircling 師troops 必must 闕watchtower,
窮Poor 寇pillage 勿do not 迫force,
此Here 用use 兵war之's 法method 也also.

Use discipline to await the chaos of battle.
Keep relaxed to await a crisis.
This is how you master emotion.

Stay close to home to await a distant enemy.
Stay comfortable to await the weary enemy.
Stay well fed to await the hungry enemy.
This is how you master power.

Don't entice the enemy when their ranks are orderly.
You must not attack when their formations are solid
This is how you master adaptation.
You must follow these military rules.
Do not take a position facing the high ground.
Do not oppose those with their backs to wall.
Do not follow those who pretend to flee.
Do not attack the enemy's strongest men.
Do not swallow the enemy's bait.
Do not block an army that is heading home.
Leave an escape outlet for a surrounded army.
Do not press a desperate foe.
This is the art of war.

九Nine 變Changes 篇Chapter

孫Sun 子Tzu 曰said:
凡All 用use 兵war之's 法methods,
將General 受endure 命order 於from 君monarch,
合Join 軍army 聚masses 眾crowd;
圮Ruined 地ground 無without 舍sheltering,
衢Highway 地ground 交join 和harmony,
絕Break off 地ground 無without 留delay,
圍Encircling 地ground 則then 謀scheme,
死Death 地ground 則then 戰battle,
途Road 有has 所place 不not 由from,
軍Army 有has 所place 不not 擊fight,
城City 有has 所place 不not 攻attack,
地Ground 有has 所place 不not 爭conflict,
君Monarch 命command 有has 所place 不not 受accept.

故Make 將general 通expert 於to 九nine 變changes 之of
利advantage 者one,
知Know 用use 兵war 矣will.

66

ADAPTABILITY

Sun Tzu said:

Everyone uses the arts of war.
As a general, you get your orders from the government.
You gather your troops.
On dangerous ground, you must not camp.
Where the roads intersect, you must join your allies.
When an area is cut off, you must not delay in it.
When you are surrounded, you must scheme.
In a life-of-death situation, you must fight.
There are roads that you must not take.
There are armies that you must not fight.
There are strongholds that you must not attack.
There are positions that you must not defend.
There are government commands that must not be obeyed.

Military leaders must be experts in knowing how to adapt to win.
This will teach you the use of war.

將Generals 不not 通expert 於to 九nine 變changes 之of 利advantage 者one,
雖Although 知know 地ground 形shape,
不No 能can 得obtain 地ground之's 利advantage 矣will.

治Govern 兵war 不not 知know 九nine 變changes 之of 術technique,
雖Although 知know 地ground 利advantage,
不Not 得obtain 人men之's 用use 矣will.

是Right 故make 智wisdom 之of 者one 慮plan,
必Must 雜variety 於to 利advantage 害disadvantage,
雜Variety 於to 利advantage 而and yet 務duties 可can 信trust 也also,
雜Variety 於to 害disadvantage 而and yet 患problems 可can 解solve 也also.

是Right 故make 屈bend 諸various 侯noblemen 者one 以by means of 害disadvantages,
役Military service 諸various 侯noblemen 者one 以by means of 業industry,
趨Hurry 諸various 侯noblemen 者one 以by means of 利advantage.

Some commanders are not good at making adjustments to
find an advantage.
They can know the shape of the terrain.
Still, they can not find an advantageous position.

Some military commanders do not know how to adjust their
methods.
They can find an advantageous position.
Still, they can not use their men effectively.

You must be creative in your planning.
You must adapt to your opportunities and weaknesses.
You can use a variety of approaches and still have a
consistent result.
You must adjust to a variety of problems and consistently
solve them.

You can deter your potential enemy by using his weaknesses
against him.
You can keep your enemy's army busy by giving it work to
do.
You can rush your enemy by offering him an advantageous
position.

故Make 用use 兵war 者one,
無Without 恃rely on 其this 不no 來meeting,
恃Rely on 吾our 有having 以by means of 待waiting 之it;
無Without 恃rely on 其this 不no 攻attack,
恃Rely on 吾our 有having 所place 不no 可can 攻attack
也also.

故Make 將general 有have 五five 危dangers:
必Must 死die 可can 殺kill,
必Must 生born 可can 虜capture,
忿Angry 速speed,
可Can 侮humiliate 也also;
廉Honest 潔clean 可can 辱disgrace,
愛Love 民people 可can 煩trouble;
凡All 此this 五five 危dangers,
將General 之's 過mistake 也also,
用Use 兵war 災disaster 也also.

覆Overturn 軍army 殺kill 將general,
必Must 以by means of 五five 危dangers,
不No 可can 不no 察examine 也also.

You must make use of war.
Do not trust that the enemy isn't coming.
Trust on your readiness to meet him.
Do not trust that the enemy won't attack.
We must rely only on our ability to pick a place that the enemy can't attack.

You can exploit five different faults in a leader.
If he is willing to die, you can kill him.
If he wants to survive, you can capture him.
He may have a quick temper.
You can then provoke him with insults.
If he has a delicate sense of honor, you can disgrace him.
If he loves his people, you can create problems for him.
In every situation, look for these five weaknesses.
They are common faults in commanders.
They always lead to military disaster.

To overturn an army, you must kill its general.
To do this, you must use these five weaknesses.
You must always look for them.

行MARCH 軍ARMY 篇Chapter

孫Sun 子Tzu 曰said:
凡All 處handle 軍army 相examine 敵enemy:

絕Break off 山mountain 依depend on 谷valley,
視Watch 生birth 處position 高high,
戰Battle 隆glorious 無without 登climb,
此Here 處position 山mountain 之of 軍army 也also.

絕Sever 水water 必must 遠distant 水water;
客Guest 絕sever 水water 而and yet 來arrive,
勿Do not 迎meet 於to 水water 內inside,
令Command 半half 濟ford river 而and yet 擊win 之of
利advantage.

欲Want 戰battle 者one,
無Without 附attaching 於at 水water 而and yet 迎meet
客guest,
視Show 生birth 處position 高high,
無Without 迎meet 水water 流flow,
此Here 處position 水water 上up 之of 軍army 也also.

Armed March

Sun Tzu said:

Everyone moving their army must adjust to the enemy.

Keep out of the mountains and in the valleys.
Position yourself on the heights facing the sun.
To win your battles, never attack uphill.
This is how you position your army in the mountains.

When water blocks you, keep far away from it.
Let the enemy cross the river and wait for him.
Do not meet him in midstream.
Wait for him to get half his forces across and then take
advantage of the situation.

You need to be able to fight.
You can't do that if you are in the water when you meet an
attack.
Position yourself upstream, facing the sun.
Never face against the current.
Always position your army upstream when near the water.

絕Break off 斥expand 澤pond,
惟However 亟urgently 去go 勿do not 留stay,
若If 交meet 軍army 於at 斥expand 澤pond之's 中middle,
必Must 依depend on 水water 草grass,
而And yet 背back 眾crowd 樹tree,
此Here 處position 斥expand 澤pond之's 軍army 也also.

平Level 陸plateau 處position 易change,
右Right 背back 高high,
前Front 死die 後behind 生born,
此Here 處position 平level 陸plateau 之of 軍army 也also.

凡All 此here 四four 軍army之's 利advantage,
黃Yellow 帝emperor之's 所place 以by means of 勝victory
四four 帝emperor 也also.

凡All 軍army 好good 高high 而and yet 惡bad 下below,
貴Sufficient 陽south, sunny hillside 而and yet 賤deficient
陰north, shady hillside,
養Provide for 生birth 而and yet 處position 實substantial,
軍Army 無without 百hundred 疾diseases,
是Correct 謂meaning 必must 勝victory.

邱Town 陵high mound 隄dike 防prevent,
必Must 處position 其this 陽south sunny hillside,
而And yet 右right 背back 之go.

此Here 軍army之's 利advantage,
地Ground之's 助assistance 也also.

You may have to move across marshes.
Move through them quickly without stopping.
You may meet the enemy in the middle of a marsh.
You must keep on the water grasses.
Keep your back to a clump of trees.
This is how you position your army in a marsh.

On a level plateau, take a position that you can change.
Keep the higher ground on your right and to the rear.
Keep the danger in front of you and safety behind.
This is how you position yourself on a level plateau.

You can find an advantage in all four of these situations.
Learn from the great emperor who used positioning to
conquer his four rivals.

Armies are stronger on high ground and weaker on low.
They are better camping on sunny, southern hillsides than on
the shady, northern ones.
Provide for your army's health and place it well.
Your army will be free from disease.
Done correctly, this means victory.

You must sometimes defend on a hill or riverbank.
You must keep on the south side in the sun.
Keep the uphill slope at your right rear.

This will give the advantage to your army.
It will always give you a position of strength.

上Above 雨rain 水water 沫tip 至stop,
欲Desire 涉ford 者one,
待Wait 其this 定decide 也also.

凡All 地ground 有have 絕break off 澗mountain stream,
天Heaven 井well,
天Heaven 牢jail,
天Heaven 羅net,
天Heaven 陷submerge,
天Heaven 隙crevice,
必Must 亟urgently 去remove 之it,
勿Do not 近near 也also;
吾We 遠distant 之it,
敵Enemy 近near 之it;
吾We 迎face 之it,
敵Enemy 背back 之it.

軍Army 旁side 有have 險danger 阻block,
潢Reservoir 井well,
蒹Reed 葭bulrush,
林Forest 木wood,
翳Screen 薈vegetation 者one,
必Must 謹caution 覆overturn 索exact 之it,
此Here 伏hide 姦seduce 也of 所place 也also.

Stop the march when the rain swells the river into rapids.
You may want to ford the river.
Wait until it subsides.

All regions have dead-ends such as waterfalls.
There are deep lakes.
There are high cliffs.
There are dense jungles.
There are thick quagmires.
There are steep crevasses.
Get away from all these quickly.
Do not get close to them.
Keep them at a distance.
Maneuver the enemy close to them.
Position yourself facing these dangers.
Push the enemy back into them.

Danger can hide on your army's flank.
There are reservoirs and lakes.
There are reeds and thickets.
There are forests of trees.
Their dense vegetation provides a hiding place.
You must cautiously search through them.
They can always hide an ambush.

敵Enemy 近near 而and yet 靜tranquil 者one,
恃Depend on 其this 險obstruction 也also,
遠Distant 而and yet 挑choose 戰battle 者one,
欲Want 人men也's 進advance 也also.

其This 所place 居reside 易change 者one,
利Advantage 也also.

眾Crowd 樹tree 動moves 者one,
來Come 也also;
眾Crowd 草grass 多many 障obstruct 者one,
疑Doubt 也also.

鳥Bird 起rise 者one,
伏 Hide 也also;
獸Beast 駭startle 者one,
覆Overturn 也also.

塵Dust:
高High 而and yet 銳sharp 者one,
車Cart 來come 也also;
卑Low 而and yet 廣wide 者one,
徒Foot 來come 也also;
散Scattered 而and yet 條linear 達reach 者one,
樵Wood 採gathered 也also;
少Little 而and yet 往toward 來coming 者one,
營encampment 軍army 也also.

Sometimes, the enemy is close by but remains calm.
Expect to find him in a natural stronghold.
Other times, he remains at a distance but provokes battle.
He wants you to attack him.

He sometimes shifts the position of his camp.
He is looking for an advantageous position.

The trees in the forest move.
Expect that the enemy is coming.
The tall grasses obstruct your view.
Be suspicious.

The birds take flight.
Expect that the enemy is hiding.
Animals startle.
Expect an ambush.

Notice the dust.
It sometimes rises high in a straight line.
Vehicles are coming.
The dust appears low in a wide band.
Foot soldiers are coming.
The dust seems scattered in different areas.
The enemy is collecting firewood.
Any dust is light and settling down.
The enemy is setting up camp.

ARMED MARCH

辭Words 卑low 而and yet 益increase 備prepare 者one,
進Advance 也also.

辭Words 強strong 而and yet 進advance 驅expel 者one,
退Retreat 也also.

輕Light 車carts 先first 出exit 居residence 其this 側side
者one,
陣Battle formation 也also.

無Without 約appointment 而and yet 請request 和peace
者one,
謀Scheme 也also.

奔Run 走depart 而and yet 陳display 兵army 者one,
期Expect 也also.

半Half 進advance 而and 半half 退retreat 者one,
誘Bait 也also.

仗Fight 而and yet 立stand 者one,
飢Starving 也also.

汲Draw 而and yet 先first 飲drink 者one,
渴Thirsty 也also.

見See 利advantage 而and yet 不 no 進advance 者one,
勞Weary 也also.

鳥Birds 集assemble 者one,
虛Empty 也also.

80

Your enemy speaks humbly while building up forces.
He is planning to advance.

The enemy talks aggressively and pushes as if to advance.
He is planning to retreat.

Small vehicles exit his camp first and move to positions on
the army's flanks.
They are forming a battle line.

Your enemy tries to sue for peace but without offering a
treaty.
He is plotting.

Your enemy's men run to leave and yet form ranks.
You should expect action.

Half his army advances and the other half retreats.
He is luring you.

Your enemy plans to fight but his men just stand there.
They are starving.

Those who draw water drink it first.
They are thirsty.

Your enemy sees an advantage but does not advance.
His men are tired.

Birds gather.
Your enemy has abandoned his camp.

夜Night 呼call 者one,
恐Fear 也also.

軍Army 擾disturb 者one,
將General 不no 重serious 也also.

旌Flags 旗banners 動move 者one,
亂Disorder 也also.

吏Official 怒angry 者one,
倦Exhausted 也also.

殺Kill 馬horse 肉meat 食food 者one,
軍Army 無without 糧provisions 也also.

懸Hang 缶crock 不no 返return 其this 舍hut 者one,
窮Poor 寇robber 也also.

諄Earnest 諄earnest 翕agreeable 翕agreeable,
徐Slow 與give 人men 言words 者one,
失Lose 眾crowd 也also.

數Number 賞reward 者one,
窘Distressed 也also.

數Number 罰penalize 者one,
困Tired 也also.

先First 暴violent 而and yet 後afterward 畏fear 其this
眾crowd 者one,
不No 精select之's 至arrive 也also.

82

Your enemy's soldiers call in the night.
They are afraid.

Your enemy's army is raucous.
They do not take their commander seriously.

Your enemy's banners and flags shift.
Order is breaking down.

Your enemy's officers are irritable.
They are exhausted.

Your enemy's men kill their horses for meat.
They are out of provisions.

They don't put their pots away or return to their tents.
They expect to fight to the death.

Enemy troops appear sincere and agreeable.
But their men are slow to speak to each other.
They are no longer united.

Your enemy offers too many incentives to his men.
He is in trouble.

Your enemy gives out too many punishments.
His men are weary.

Your enemy first attacks and then is afraid of your larger
force.
His best troops have not arrived.

來Meet 委committee 謝thank 者one,
欲Desire 休rest 息breath 也also.

兵War 怒fury 而and yet 相appears 迎greet,
久Long time 而and yet 不no 合join,
又Both 不no 相appear 去go,
必Must 謹cautious 察examine 之it.

兵War 非weak 益augment 多many,
惟However 無without 武troops 進advance,
足Sufficient 以by means of 併side-by-side 力power 料expect
敵enemy 取obtain 人men 而and yet 已stop.

夫Husband 惟consider 無without 慮plan 而and yet 易change
敵enemy 者one,
必Must 擒capture 於to 人men.

卒Soldier 未not yet 親intimate 附depend on 而and yet
罰penalize 之it,
則Then 不no 服obey,
不No 服obey 則then 難difficult 用use.

卒Soldier 已finished 親intimate 附depend on,
而And yet 罰penalize 不no 行act,
則Then 不no 可can 用use.

故Make 令commands 之it 以by means of 文culture,
齊Together 之it 以by means of 武conquest,
是Right 謂meaning 必must 取obtain.

Your enemy comes in a conciliatory manner.
He needs to rest and recuperate.

Your enemy is angry and appears to welcome battle.
This goes on for a long time, but he doesn't attack.
He also doesn't leave the field.
You must watch him carefully.

If you are too weak to fight, you must find more men.
In this situation, you must not act aggressively.
You must unite your forces, expect the enemy, recruit men
and wait.

You must be cautious about making plans and adjust to the
enemy.
You must increase the size of your forces.

With new, undedicated soldiers, you can depend on them if
you discipline them.
They will tend to disobey your orders.
If they do not obey your orders, they will be useless.

You can depend on seasoned, dedicated soldiers.
But you must avoid disciplining them without reason.
Otherwise, you cannot use them.

You must control your soldiers with *esprit de corp*.
You must bring them together by winning victories.
You must get them to believe in you.

令Command 素simple 行march 以by means of 教teaching
其these 民people,
則Then 民people 服obey;
令Command 不no 素simple 行march 以by means of
教teaching 其these 民people,
則Then 民people 不no 服obey.

令Command 素simple 行march,
與Give 眾crowd 相study 得obtain 也also.

Make it easy for them to obey your orders by training your people.
Your people will then obey you.
If you do not make it easy to obey, you won't train your people.
Then they will not obey.

Make your commands easy to follow.
You must understand the way a crowd thinks.

地GROUND 形FORM 篇Chapter

孫Sun 子Tzu 曰said:
地Ground 形form 有has 通unobstructed 者one,
有Has 挂hanging 者one,
有Has 支support 者one,
有Has 隘confined 者one,
有Has 險obstructed 者one,
有Has 遠distant 者one.

我I 可can 以by means of 往depart,
彼Mutually 可can 以by means of 來join,
曰Say 通unobstructed;
通Unobstructed 形form 者thing,
先First 居live 高high 陽south, sunny hillside,
利Advantage 糧provisions 道way 以by means of 戰battle,
則Then 利advantage.

FIELD POSITION

Sun Tzu said:

Some field positions are unobstructed.
Some field positions are entangling.
Some field positions are supporting.
Some field positions are constricted.
Some field positions give you a barricade.
Some field positions are spread out.

You can attack from some positions easily.
Others can attack you easily as well.
We call these unobstructed positions.
These positions are open.
On them, be the first to occupy a high, sunny area.
Put yourself where you can defend your supply routes.
Then you will have an advantage.

可Can 以by means of 往depart,
難Disaster 以by means of 返return,
曰Say 挂suspended;
挂Suspended 形form 者thing,
敵Enemy 無without 備preparation,
出Exit 而and yet 勝win 之it,
敵Enemy 若seems 有have 備preparation,
出Exit 而and yet 不no 勝win,
難Disaster 以by means of 返return,
不No 利advantage.

我I 出exit 而and yet 不no 利advantage,
彼Each other 出exit 而and yet 不no 利advantage,
曰Say 支support;
支Support 形form 者thing,
敵Enemy 雖through 利advantage 我I;
我I 無without 出exit 也also;
引Pull 而and yet 去remove 之it,
令Command 敵enemy 半half 出exit 而but 擊strike 之it,
利Advantage.

隘Narrow 形form 者thing,
我I 先first 居dwell 之it,
必Must 盈fill 之it 以by means of 待awaiting 敵enemy,
若Seem 敵enemy 先first 居dwell 之it,
盈Full 而and yet 勿do not 從follow,
不Not 盈full 而and yet 從follow 之it.

90

You can attack from some positions easily.
Disaster arises when you try to return to them.
These are entangling positions.
These field positions are one-sided.
Wait until your enemy is unprepared.
You can then attack from these positions and win.
Avoid a well prepared enemy.
You will try to attack and lose.
Since you can't return, you will meet disaster.
These field positions offer no advantage.

I cannot leave some positions without losing an advantage.
If the enemy leaves this ground, he also loses an advantage.
We call these supporting field positions.
These positions strengthen you.
The enemy may try to entice me away.
Still, I will hold my position.
You must entice the enemy to leave.
You then strike him as he is leaving.
These field positions offer an advantage.

Some field positions are constricted.
I try to get to these positions before the enemy does.
You must fill these areas and await the enemy.
Sometimes, the enemy will reach them first.
If he fills them, do not follow him.
However, if he fails to fill them, you can go after him.

險Obstructed 形form 者thing:
我I 先first 居dwell 之it,
必Must 居reside 高high 陽south, sunny hillside
以by means of 待await 敵enemy,
若Seem 敵enemy 先first 居dwell 之it,
引Pull 而and yet 去remove 之it,
勿Do not 從follow 也also.

遠Distant 形form 者thing,
勢Force 均fair,
難Disaster 以by means of 挑choose 戰battle,
戰Battle 而and yet 不no 利advantage.

凡All 此these 六six 者things,
地Ground之's 道philosophy 也also,
將General之's 至arrival 任assignment,
不No 可can 不no 察examine 也also.

故Make 兵wars 有have 走move 者thing,
有Have 弛relax 者thing,
有Have 陷sink 者thing,
有Have 崩collapse 者thing,
有Have 亂disorder 者thing,
有Have 北flee 者thing.

凡All 此these 六six 者things,
非Weak 天heaven 地ground之's 災disaster,
將General之's 過pass 也also.

92

Some field positions give you a barricade.
I get to these positions before the enemy does.
You occupy their southern, sunny heights and wait for the
enemy.
Sometimes the enemy occupies these areas first.
If so, entice him away.
Never go after him.

Some field positions are too spread out.
Your force may seem equal to the enemy.
Still you will lose if you provoke a battle.
If you fight, you will not have any advantage.

These are the six types of field positions.
Each battleground has its own rules.
As a commander, you must know where to go.
You must examine each position closely.

Some armies can be outmaneuvered.
Some armies are too lax.
Some armies fall down.
Some armies fall apart.
Some armies are disorganized.
Some armies must retreat.

Know all six of these weaknesses.
They lead to losses on both good and bad ground.
They all arise from the army's commander.

夫Husband 勢force 均equal,
以By means of 一one 擊strike 十ten,
曰Say 走move.

吏Officers 弱weak 卒soldiers 強strong,
曰Say 弛relax.

卒Soldiers 強strong 吏officers 弱weak,
曰Say 陷sink.

大Big 吏officers 怒rage 而and yet 不no 服obey,
遇Meet 敵enemy 懟hate 而and yet 自self 戰battle,
將General 不no 知knowledge 其this 能can,
曰Say 崩collapse.

將General 弱weak 不not 嚴strict,
教Teach 道philosophy 不not 明clear,
吏Officers 卒soldiers 無without 常rule,
陳Show 兵war 縱vertical 橫horizontal,
曰Say 亂disorder.

將General 不no 能can 料predict 敵enemy,
以By means of 少few 合join 眾crowd,
以By means of 弱weak 擊strike 強strong,
兵War 無without 選choice 鋒sword point,
曰Say 北flee.

凡All 此these 六six 者things,
敗Defeat之's 道philosophy 也also,
將General之's 至arrive 任allow,
不No 能can 不no 察examine 也also.

94

One general can command a force equal to the enemy.
Still his enemy outflanks him.
This means that his army can be outmaneuvered.

Another can have strong soldiers, but weak officers.
This means that his army will be too lax.

Another has strong officers but weak soldiers.
This means that his army will fall down.

Another has sub-commanders that are angry and defiant.
They attack the enemy and fight their own battles.
As a commander, he cannot know the battlefield.
This means that his army will fall apart.

Another general is weak and easygoing.
He fails to make his orders clear.
His officers and men lack direction,
This shows in his military formations.
This means that his army will be disorganized.

Another general fails to predict the enemy.
He pits his small forces against larger ones.
He puts his weak forces against stronger ones.
He fails to pick his fights correctly.
This means that his army must retreat.

You must know all about these six weaknesses.
You must understand the philosophies that lead to defeat.
When a general arrives, you can know what he will do.
You must study each one carefully.

夫Husband 地ground 形form 者thing,
兵War之's 助assistance 也also.

料Predict 敵enemy 制overpower 勝victory,
計Plan 險obstructed 阨adverse 遠distant 近near,
上Above 將general之's 道philosophy 也also.

知Know 此this 而and yet 用use 戰battle 者one,
必Must 勝win,
不Not 知know 此this 而and yet 用use 戰battle 者one,
必Must 敗be defeated.

故Make 戰battle 道philosophy 必must 勝win;
主Master 曰say:
無Without 戰battle;
必Must 戰battle 可can 也also.

戰Battle 道philosophy 不no 勝victory,
主Master 曰say 必must 戰battle,
無Without 戰battle 可can 也also.

故Make 進advance 不no 求seek 名fame,
退Retreat 不no 避evade 罪crime,
唯Only 民people 是correct 保preserve,
而And yet 利advantage 於to 主master,
國Nation之's 寶treasure 也also.

You must control your field position.
It will always strengthen your army.

You must predict the enemy to overpower him and win.
You must analyze the obstacles, dangers, and distances.
This is the best way to command.

Understand your field position before you go to battle.
Then you will win.
You can fail to understand your field position and still fight.
Then you will lose.

You must provoke battle when you will certainly win.
It doesn't matter what you are ordered.
The government may order you not to fight.
Despite that, you must always fight when you will win.

Sometimes provoking a battle will lead to a loss.
The government may order you to fight.
Despite that, you must avoid battle when you will lose.

You must advance without desiring praise.
You must retreat without fearing shame.
The only correct move is to preserve your troops.
This is how you serve your country.
This is how you reward your nation.

視Consider 卒soldier 如comparable to 嬰infant 兒son,
故Make 可can 與give 之of 赴attend 深deep 谿brook,
視Consider 卒soldier 如comparable to 愛love 子child,
故Make 可can 與give 之of 俱all 死death.

厚Generous 而and yet 不no 能can 使use,
愛Love 而and yet 不no 能can 令command,
亂Disorder 而and yet 不no 能can 治govern,
譬Compare 若seem 驕proud 子child,
不No 能can 可use 也also.

知Know 吾our 卒soldiers 之's 可can 以by 擊strike,
而And yet 不no 知know 敵enemy 之's 不no 可can 擊strike,
勝Victory 之of 半half 也also;
知Know 敵enemy 之's 可can 擊strike,
而And yet 不no 知know 吾our 卒soldiers 之's 不no 可can
以by means of 擊strike,
勝Victory 之of 半half 也also;
知Know 敵enemy 之's 可can 擊strike,
知Know 吾our 卒soldiers 之's 可can 以by 擊strike,
而And yet 不no 知know 地earth 形form 之's 不no 可can
以by means of 戰battle,
勝Victory 之of 半half 也also.

故Make 知know 兵war 者one,
動Act 而and yet 不no 迷confusions,
舉Lift 而and yet 不no 窮limit.

Think of your soldiers as little children.
You can make them follow you into a deep river.
Treat them as your beloved children.
You can lead them all to their deaths.

Some leaders are generous, but cannot use their men.
They love their men, but cannot command them.
Their men are unruly and disorganized.
These leaders create spoiled children.
Their soldiers are useless.

You may know what your soldiers will do in an attack.
You may not know if the enemy is vulnerable to attack.
You will then win only half the time.
You may know that the enemy is vulnerable to attack.
You may not know if your men are capable of attacking them.
You will still win only half the time.
You may know that the enemy is vulnerable to attack.
You may know that your men are ready to attack.
You may not know how to position yourself in the field for battle.
You will still win only half the time.

You must know how to make war.
You can then act without confusion.
You can attempt anything.

故Make 曰say:
知Know 彼each other 知know 己self,
勝Victory 乃consequently 不no 殆dangerous,
知Know 天heaven 知know 地earth,
勝Victory 乃consequently 可can 全complete.

We say:
Know the enemy and know yourself.
Your victory will be painless.
Know the weather and the field.
Your victory will be complete.

九NINE 地GROUND 篇Chapter

孫Sun 子Tzu 曰said:
用Use 兵war之's 法methods,
有Have 散scattered 地ground,
有Have 輕easy 地ground,
有Have 爭contended 地ground,
有Have 交meeting 地ground,
有Have 衢highway 地ground,
有Have 重serious 地ground,
有Have 圮destroyed 地ground,
有Have 圍surround 地ground,
有Have 死death 地ground.

諸Various 侯noblemen 自self 戰battle 其this 地ground 者one,
為Become 散scattered 地ground.

入Enter 人men 之's 地ground 不no 深deep 者one,
為Become 輕easy 地ground.

我I 得get 則then 利advantage,
彼Others 得get 亦also 利advantage 者one,
為Become 爭contended 地ground.

102

Types of Terrain

Sun Tzu said:

Use the art of war.
Know when the terrain will scatter you.
Know when the terrain will be easy.
Know when the terrain will be disputed.
Know when the terrain is open.
Know when the terrain is intersecting.
Know when the terrain is dangerous.
Know when the terrain is bad.
Know when the terrain is confined.
Know when the terrain is deadly.

Warring parties must sometimes fight inside their own
territory.
This is scattering terrain.

When you enter hostile territory, your penetration is shallow.
This is easy terrain.

Some terrain gives me an advantageous position.
But it gives others an advantageous position as well.
This will be disputed terrain.

我I 可can 以be means of 往go forward,
彼Others 可can 以by means of 來join 者one,
為Becomes 交meeting 地ground.

諸Various 侯noblemen之's 地ground 三three 屬belong,
先First 至arrive 而and yet 得obtain 天heaven 下below
眾crowd 者one,
為Becomes 衢highway 地ground.

入Enter 人men之's 地ground 深deeply,
背Behind 城citadel 邑town 多many 者one,
為Becomes 重serious 地ground.

山Mountain 林forest,
險Dangerous 阻obstruction,
沮Prevent 澤pond,
凡All 難disaster 行march之's 道way 者one,
為Becomes 圮destroyed 地ground.

所Place 由from 入enter 者one 隘narrow,
所Place 從follow 歸return 者one 迂close-in,
彼Other 寡few 可can 以by means of 擊strike 吾we 之of
眾crowd 者one,
為Become 圍surround 地ground.

疾Swift 戰battle 則then 存exist,
不No 疾swift 戰battle 則then 亡die 存one,
為Become 死death 地ground.

I can use some terrain to advance easily.
Others can advance along with us.
This is open terrain.

Everyone shares access to a given area.
The first one there can gather a larger group than anyone else.
This is intersecting terrain.

You can penetrate deeply into hostile territory.
Then many hostile cities are behind you.
This is dangerous terrain.

There are mountain forests.
There are rugged hills.
There are marshes.
Everyone confronts these obstacles on a campaign.
They make bad terrain.

In some areas, the passage is narrow.
You are closed in as you enter and exit them.
In this type of area, a few people can attack our much larger force.
This is confined terrain.

You can sometimes survive only if you fight quickly.
You will die if you delay.
This is deadly terrain.

是Correct 故make 散scattered 地ground 則then 無without 戰battle,
輕Easy 地ground 則then 無without 止stopping,
爭Contended 地ground 則then 無without 攻attacking,
交Meeting 地ground 則then 無without 絕breaking off,
衢Highway 地ground 則then 交meet 和harmony,
重Serious 地ground 則then 掠plunder,
圮Destroyed 地ground 則then 行march,
圍Surround 地ground 則then 謀scheme,
死Death 地ground 則then 戰battle.

☯

故Make 之go 所place 謂call 善friendly 用use 兵war 者one,
能Can 使use 敵enemy 人men 前forward 後behind 不no 相examine 及attain,
眾Crowd 寡few 不no 相study 恃depend on,
貴Sufficient 賤deficient 不no 相study 救rescue,
上Above 下below 不no 相study 收gather,
卒Soldier 離leave 而and yet 不no 集assembly,
兵War 合join 而and yet 不no 齊order.

合Join 於to 利advantage 而and yet 動move,
不No 合join 於to 利advantage 而and yet 止stop.

敢Daring 問asks:
"敵Enemy 眾crowd 整orderly 而and yet 將general 來arrive,
待Wait 之it 若if 何what?"

106

To be successful, you control scattering terrain by not fighting.
Control easy terrain by not stopping.
Control disputed terrain by not attacking.
Control open terrain by staying with the enemy's forces.
Control intersecting terrain by uniting with your allies.
Control dangerous terrain by plundering.
Control bad terrain by keeping on the move.
Control confined terrain by using surprise.
Control deadly terrain by fighting.

Go to an area that helps you in waging war.
Use it to cut off the enemy's contact between his front and back lines.
Prevent his small parties from relying on his larger force.
Stop his strong divisions from rescuing his weak ones.
Prevent his officers from getting his men together.
Chase his soldiers apart to stop them from amassing.
Harass them to prevent their ranks from forming.

When joining battle gives you an advantage, you must do it.
When it isn't to your benefit, you must avoid it.

A daring soldier may ask:
"A large, organized enemy army and its general are coming.
 What do I do to prepare for them?"

曰Say:
"先First 奪seize 其this 所place 愛love,
則Then 聽listen 矣will;
兵Army 之's 情essence 主master 速speed,
乘Ride 人men 之's 不no 及attain,
由From 不no 虞problems 之's 道philosophy,
攻Attack 其this 所place 不no 戒guard 也also."

凡All 為become 客guest 之's 道philosophy,
深Deeply 入enter 則then 專concentrate,
主Master 人men 不no 克repress.

掠Plunder 於to 饒abundant 野countryside,
三Three 軍armies 足sufficient 食provisions.

謹Caution 養raise 而and yet 無without 勞weariness,
併Side-by-side 氣spirit 積accumulates 力force,
運Transport 兵war 計plans 謀scheme,
為Become 不no 可can 測measure,
投Throw 之it 無without 所place 往depart for,
死Dead 且and 不no 北flee,
死Dead 焉how 不no 得obtain,
士Officer 人men 盡exhaust 力power.

兵War 士officers 甚very 甚sink 則then 不no 甚dread,
無Without 所place 往depart for 則then 固sturdy,
深Deep 入enter 則then 拘arrest,
不No 得obtain 已finish 則then 鬥struggle.

Tell him:
"First seize an area that the enemy must have.
  Then they will pay attention to you.
  Mastering speed is the essence of war.
  Take advantage of a large enemy's inability to keep up.
  Use a philosophy of avoiding difficult situations.
  Attack the area where he doesn't expect you."

You must use the philosophy of an invader.
Invade deeply and then concentrate your forces.
This controls your men without oppressing them.

Get your supplies from the riches of the territory.
It is sufficient to supply your whole army.

Take care of your men and do not overtax them.
Your *esprit de corps* increases your momentum.
Keep your army moving and plan for surprises.
Make it difficult for the enemy to count your forces.
Position your men where there is no place to run.
They will then face death without fleeing.
They will find a way to survive.
Your officers and men will fight to their utmost.

Military officers that are committed lose their fear.
When they have nowhere to run, they must stand firm.
Deep in enemy territory, they are captives.
Since they cannot escape, they will fight.

是Correct 故make,
其This 兵war 不no 修fix 而and yet 戒guard against,
不No 求strive for 而and yet 得obtain,
不No 約bind 而and yet 親intimate,
不No 令command 而and yet 信trust.

禁Prohibit 祥guessing 去remove 疑doubt,
至Stop 死death 無without 所place 之go.

吾Our 士officer 無without 餘excess 財wealth,
非Not 惡evil 貨money 也also;
無Without 餘excess 命life,
非Not 惡evil 壽longevity 也also.

令Command 發launch之's 日day,
士Officers 卒soldiers 坐sit 者one 涕tears 霑moisten 襟lapel,
偃Cease 臥lie down 者one 涕tears 交join 頤cheeks,
投Toss 之it 無without 所place 往depart for,
則Then 諸various 劌cut之's 勇brave 也also.

☯

故Make **M**ake 善good 用use 兵war 者one,
譬Compare 如like 率instant 然reflex,
率Instant 然reflex 者one,
常Ordinary 山mountain之's 蛇snake 也also,
擊Strike 其this 首head,
則Then 尾tail 至arrive,
擊Strike 其this 尾tail,
則Then 首head 至arrive,
擊Strike 其this 中middle,
則Then 首head 尾tail 俱all 至arrive.

110

Commit your men completely.
Without being posted, they will be on guard.
Without being asked, they will get what is needed.
Without being forced, they will be dedicated.
Without being given orders, they can be trusted.

Stop them from guessing by removing all their doubts.
Stop them from dying by giving them no place to run.

Your officers may not be rich.
Nevertheless, they still desire plunder.
They may die young.
Nevertheless, they still want to live forever.

You must order the time of attack.
Officers and men may sit and weep until their lapels are wet.
When they stand up, tears may stream down their cheeks.
Put them in a position where they cannot run.
They will show the greatest courage under fire.

Make good use of war.
This demands instant reflexes.
You must develop these instant reflexes.
Act like an ordinary mountain snake.
Someone can strike at your head.
You can then attack with your tail
Someone can strike at your tail.
You can then attack with your head.
Someone can strike at your middle.
You can then attack with both your head and tail.

111

敢Daring 問asks:
"兵War 可can 使use 如like 率swift 然snake?"
曰Say:
"可Can."

夫Husband 吳boast 人men 與give 越exceed 人men
相examine 惡hate 也also.
當Regard as 其this 同together 舟boat 濟ford river 而and yet
遇meet 風wind,
其This 相study 救rescue 也also 如comparable to 左left
右right 手hand.

是Correct 故make,
方Region 馬horse 埋bury 輪wheels,
未Not yet 足sufficient 恃depend on 也also,
齊Orderly 勇brave 如compare to 一one,
政Government之's 道philosophy 也also;
剛Tough 柔tender 皆together 得obtain,
地Ground之's 理management 也also.

故Make 善good 用use 兵war 者one,
攜Carry 手hand 若seem 使use 一one 人man,
不No 得obtain 已finish 也also.

將General 軍army之's 事profession,
靜Tranquil 以by means of 幽secluded,
正Proper 以by mean of 治rule,
能Can 愚fool 士officers 卒soldiers之's 耳ear 目eye,
使Use 之it 無without 知knowledge.

A daring soldier asks:
"Can any army imitate these instant reflexes?"
We answer:
"It can."

To command and get the most of proud people, you must
study adversity.
People work together when they are in the same boat during
a storm.
In this situation, one rescues the other just as the right hand
helps the left.

Use adversity correctly.
Tether your horses and bury your wagon's wheels.
Still, you can't depend on this alone.
An organized force is braver than lone individuals.
This is the art of organization.
Put the tough and weak together.
You must also use the terrain.

Make good use of war.
Unite your men as one.
Never let them give up.

The commander must be a military professional.
This requires confidence and detachment.
You must maintain dignity and order.
You must control what your men see and hear.
They must follow you without knowing your plans.

易Change 其this 事profession,
革Transform 其this 謀scheme,
使Use 人men 無without 知knowledge.

易Change 其this 居residence,
迂Detour 其this 途road,
使Use 人men 不no 得obtain 慮strategy.

帥Commander 與give 之of 期period,
如Compare to 登climbing 高high 而and yet 去remove 其this
梯ladder,
帥Commander 與give 之of 深deep 入enter 之of 諸various
侯noblemen之's 地ground 而and yet 發launch 其this
機opportunity.

若Seem 驅expel 群herd 羊sheep.

驅Expel 而and yet 往depart,
驅Expel 而and yet 來arrive,
莫Not 知know 所place 之go,
聚Gather 三three 軍armies 之of 眾crowd,
投Throw 之of 於to 險obstruction,
此Here 將general 軍army之's 事profession 也also.

九Nine 地grounds 之of 變change,
屈Bend 伸stretch 之of 利advantage,
人Men 情love 之of 理administrate,
不No 可can 不no 察study 也also.

☯

114

You can reinvent your men's roles.
You can change your plans.
You can use your men without their understanding.

You must shift your campgrounds.
You must take detours from the ordinary routes.
You must use your men without giving them your strategy.

A commander provides what his army needs now.
You must be willing to climb high and then kick away your ladder.
You must be able to lead your men deeply into your enemy's territory and then find a way to create the opportunity that you need.

You must drive men like a flock of sheep.

You must drive them to march.
You must drive them to attack.
You must never let them know where you are headed.
You must unite them into a great army.
You must then drive them against all opposition.
This is the job of a true commander.

You must adapt to the different terrain.
You must adapt to find an advantage.
You must manage your people's affections.
You must study all these skills.

凡All 為become 客guest 之's 道philosophy,
深Deep 則then 專concentrate,
淺Shallow 則then 散scatter;
去Remove 國nation 越transverse 境boundary 而and yet
師command 者one,
絕Break off 地ground 也also;
四Four 通unobstructed 者one,
衢Highway 地ground 也also;
入Enter 深deeply 者one,
重Serious 地ground 也also;
入Enter 淺shallow 者one,
輕Easy 地ground 也also;
背Back 固walls 前front 隘narrow 者one,
圍surround 地ground 也also;
無Without 所place 往depart for 者one,
死Death 地ground 也also.

是Correct 故make 散scatter 地ground 吾our 將general
一one 其this 志ambition;
輕Easy 地ground 吾our 將general 使use 之it 屬belong;
爭Contend 地ground 吾our 將general 趨tend 其this
後fall behind,
交Meet 地ground 吾our 將general 謹cautious 其this
守defend,
衢Highway 地ground 吾our 將general 固firm 其this 結ties;
重Serious 地ground 吾our 將general 繼follow 其this 食food;
圮Ruined 地ground 吾we 將general 進advance 其this 途road;
圍Surround 地ground 吾our 將general 塞stronghold 其this
闕tower;
死Death 地ground 吾our 將general 示show 之it 以by 不no
活life.

116

Always use the philosophy of invasion.
Deep invasions concentrate your forces.
Shallow invasions scatter your forces.
When you leave your country and cross the border, you must take control.
This is always critical ground.
You can sometimes move in any direction.
This is always intersecting ground.
You can penetrate deeply into a territory.
This is always dangerous ground.
You penetrate only a little way.
This is always easy ground.
Your retreat is closed and the path ahead tight.
This is always confined ground.
There is sometimes no place to run.
This is always deadly ground.

To use scattering terrain correctly, we must inspire our men's devotion.
On easy terrain, we must keep in close communication.
On disputed terrain, we should try to hamper the enemy's progress.
On open terrain, we must carefully defend our chosen position.
On intersecting terrain, we must solidify our alliances.
On dangerous terrain, we must ensure our food supplies.
On bad terrain, we must keep advancing along the road.
On confined terrain, we must make block information flow from our headquarters.
On deadly terrain, we must show what we can do by killing the enemy.

故Make 兵war之's 情feelings,
圍Surround 則then 禦defend,
不No 得obtain 已stop 則then 鬥struggle,
逼Force 則then 從obey.

是Correct 故cause 不no 知knowledge 諸various
侯noblemen之's 謀scheme 者one,
不No 能can 預prepare 交join.

不No 知knowledge 山mountain 林forest 險difficulties
阻block 沮prevent 澤pond之's 形form 者one,
不No 能can 行march 軍army,
不No 用use 鄉countryside 導guide 者one,
不No 能can 得obtain 地ground 利advantage.

此Here 三three 者things,
不No 知knowledge 一one,
非Wrong 覇dominate 王ruler之's 兵war 也also.

夫Husband 覇dominate 王ruler之's 兵war,
伐Cutdown 大big 國nation 則then 其this 眾crowd 不no
得obtain 聚assembly,
威Fear 加increase 於to 敵enemy,
則Then 其this 交meeting 不no 得obtain 合join.

是Correct 故cause 不no 爭struggle 天heaven 下below之's
交meeting;
不No 養provide for 天heaven 下below之's 權authority,
信Trust 己self之's 私selfish,
威Fear 加increase 於to 敵enemy,
故Make 其this 城city 可can 拔pull out,
其This 國nation 可can 墮fall.

118

Make your men feel like an army.
Surround them and they will defend themselves.
If they cannot avoid it, they will fight.
If they are under pressure, they will obey.

Do the right thing when you don't know your different
enemies' plans.
Don't attempt to meet them.

You don't know the local mountains, forests, hills and
marshes?
Then you cannot march the army.
You don't have local guides?
You won't get any of the benefits of the terrain.

There are many factors in war.
You may lack knowledge of any one of them.
If so, it is wrong to take a nation into war.

You must be able to dominate a nation at war.
Divide a big nation before they are able to gather a large
force.
Increase your enemy's fear.
Prevent his forces from getting together and organizing.

Do the right thing and don't try to compete for outside
alliances.
You won't have to fight for authority.
Trust only yourself and your own resources.
This increases the enemy's uncertainty.
You can force one of his allies to pull out.
His whole nation can fall.

119

施Bestow 無without 法law 之of 賞wealth,
懸Suspend 無without 政government之's 令command,
犯Attack 三three 軍army之's 眾crowd,
若Seem 使use 一one 人man.

犯Attack 之it 以by means of 事profession,
勿Do not 告report 以by means of 言word;
犯Attack 之it 以by means of 利advantage,
勿Do not 告report 以by means of 害harm;
投Throw 之it 亡death 地ground 然however 後fall behind
存exist,
陷Shrink 之it 亡death 地ground 然however 後fall behind
生born;

夫Husband 眾crowd 陷sink 於to 害misfortune,
然However 後fall behind 能can 為become 勝victory
敗defeat,
故Make 為become 兵war之's 事profession;
在Exist 順arrange 詳in detail 敵enemy之's 意intention,
併Side by side 敵enemy 一one 向direction,
千Thousand 里miles 殺kill 將general,
是Correct 謂meaning 巧skillful 能can 成become
事profession.

☯

是Correct 故cause 政government 舉lift 之of 日day,
夷Barbarians 關close off 折break 符match,
無Without 通road 其this 使envoys,
勵Encourage 於to 廊halls 廟headquarters之's 上above,
以By mean of 誅kill 其this 事profession,
敵Enemy 人men 開open 闔close,
必Must 亟urgently 入enter 之it.

120

Distribute plunder without worrying about agreements.
Halt without the government's command.
Attack with the whole strength of your army.
Use your army as if it was a single man.

Attack with skill.
Do not discuss it.
Attack when you have an advantage.
Do not talk about the dangers.
When you can launch your army into deadly ground, even if
it stumbles, it can still survive.
You can be weakened in a deadly battle and yet be stronger
afterward.

Even a large force can fall into misfortune.
If you fall behind, however, you can still turn defeat into
victory.
You must use the skills of war.
To survive, you must adapt yourself to your enemy's purpose.
You must stay with him no matter where he goes.
It may take a thousand miles to kill the general.
If you correctly understand him, you can find the skill to do
it.

Manage your government correctly at the start of a war.
Close your borders and tear up passports.
Block the passage of envoys.
Encourage politicians at headquarters to stay out of it.
You must use any means to put an end to politics.
Your enemy's people will leave you an opening.
You must instantly invade through it.

先First 其this 所place 愛love,
微Slight 與give 之of 期period,
踐Trample 墨ink 隨follow 敵enemy,
以By means of 決decision 戰battle 事profession.

是Correct 故cause 始start 如comparably to 處position
女woman
敵Enemy 人men 開open 戶door,
後Afterwards 如comparable 脫skin 兔rabbit,
敵Enemy 不no 及attain 拒refuse.

122

Immediately seize a place that they love.
Do it quickly.
Trample any border to pursue the enemy.
Use your judgment about when to fight.

Doing the right thing at the start of war is like approaching a woman.
Your enemy's men must open the door.
After that, you should act like a streaking rabbit.
The enemy will be unable to catch you.

火FIRE 攻ATTACK 篇Chapter

孫Sun 子Tzu 曰said:
凡All 火fire 攻attacks 有have 五five:
一1. 曰Say 火fire 人men,
二2. 曰Say 火fire 積resources,
三3. 曰Say 火fire 輜supply wagons,
四4. 曰Say 火fire 庫houses,
五5. 曰Say 火fire 隊group.

行Do 火fire 必must 有have 因cause,
煙Smoke 火fire 必must 素raw 具prepare.

發Launch 火fire 有have 時season,
起Begin 火fire 有have 日day.

時Season 者one,
天Heaven之's 燥dry 也also.

日Day 者one,
月Month 在during 其grasses 壁wall 翼sides 軫cart 也also.

凡All 此here 四four 宿constellation 者one,
風Wind 起start of 日day 也also.

124

Attacking with Fire

Sun Tzu said:

There are five ways of attacking with fire.
The first is burning troops.
The second is burning supplies.
The third is burning supply transport.
The fourth is burning storehouses.
The fifth is burning camps.

To make fire, you must have the resources.
To build a fire, you must prepare the raw materials.

To attack with fire, you must be in the right season.
To start a fire, you must have the time.

Choose the right season.
The weather must be very dry.

Choose the right time.
Pick a season when the grass is as high as the side of a cart.

You can tell the proper days by the stars in the night sky.
You want days when the wind rises in the morning.

凡All 火fire 攻attacks,
必Must 因cause 五five 火fires之's 變change 而and yet
應comply with 之it.

火Fire 發launch 於to 內internal,
則Then 早early 應respond 之it 於to 外external.

火Fire 發launch 而and yet 其this 兵war 靜tranquil 者one,
待Wait 而and yet 勿do not 攻attack.

極Extreme 其this 火fire 力power,
可Can 從follow 而and yet 從follow 之it,
不No 可can 從follow 而and yet 止stop.

火Fire 可can 發distribute 於to 外external,
無Without 待wait 於to 內internal,
以By mean of 時time 發distribute 之it.

火Fire 發distribute 上upper 風wind,
無Without 攻attack 下lower 風wind,
晝Daytime 風wind 久long time,
夜Night 風wind 止stop.

凡All 軍army 必must 知know 有have 五five 火fire之's
變change,
以By means of 數several 守guard 之it.

126

Everyone attacks with fire.
You must create five different situations with fire and be able
to adjust to them.

You start a fire inside the enemy's camp.
Then attack the enemy's periphery.

You launch a fire attack, but the enemy remains calm.
Wait and do not attack.

The fire reaches its height.
Follow its path if you can.
If you can't follow it, stay where you are.

Spreading fires on the outside of camp can kill.
You can't always get fire inside the enemy's camp.
Take your time in spreading it.

Set the fire when the wind is at your back.
Don't attack into the wind.
Daytime winds last a long time.
Night winds fade quickly.

Every army must know how to deal with the five attacks by
fire.
Use many men to guard against them.

故Make 以by 火fire 佐assistance 攻attack 者one 明bright,
以By means of 水water 佐assist 攻attack 者one 強powerful
水Water 可can 以by means of 絕break-off,
不No 可can 以by means of 奪seize.

☯

夫Husband 戰battle 勝victory 攻attack 取obtain,
而And yet 不no 修study 其this 功achievement 者one
凶unlucky,
命Command 曰say 費waste 留remain.

故Cause 曰say:
明bright 主master 慮plan 之it,
良Good 將general 修study 之it,
非Weak 利advantage 不no 動act,
非Weak 得obtain 不no 用use,
非Weak 危danger 不no 戰battle.

主Ruler 不no 可can 以by means of 怒fury 而and yet
興prosper 師legion,
將General 不no 可can 以by mean of 慍anger 而and yet
致make 戰battle;
合Join 於to 利advantage 而and yet 動act,
不No 合join 於to 利advantage 而and yet 止stop.

怒Fury 可can 以by means of 復recover 喜happiness,
慍Anger 可can 以by means of 復recover 悅joy,
亡Dead 國nation 不no 可can 以by 復recover 存life,
死Dead 者one 不no 可can 以by 復recover 生birth.

128

When you use fire to assist your attacks, you are clever.
Water can add force to an attack.
You can also use water to disrupt an enemy.
It doesn't, however, take his resources.

You win in battle by getting the opportunity to attack.
It is dangerous if you fail to study how to accomplish this achievement.
As commander, you cannot waste your opportunities.

We say:
A wise leader plans success.
A good general studies it.
If there is little to be gained, don't act.
If there is little to win, do not use your men.
If there is no danger, don't fight.

As leader, you cannot let your anger interfere with the success of your forces.
As commander, you cannot fight simply because you are enraged.
Join the battle only when it is in your advantage to act.
If there is no advantage in joining a battle, stay put.

Anger can change back into happiness.
Rage can change back into joy.
A nation once destroyed cannot be brought back to life.
Dead men do not return to the living.

故Cause 明bright 主master 慎caution 之it,
良Good 將general 警warn 之it.

此Here 安peaceful 國nation 全whole 軍army之's
道philosophy 也also.

This fact must make a wise leader cautious.
A good general is on guard.

Your philosophy must be to keep the nation peaceful and the army intact.

用USE 間SPIES 篇Chapter

孫Sun 子Tzu 曰said:
凡All 興together 師troops 十ten 萬ten thousand,
出Exit 征journey 千thousand 里miles,
百Hundred 姓clans之's 費waste,
公Public 家family之's 奉offer,
日Day 費waste 千thousand 金dollars.

內Inside 外outside 騷stimulate 動act,
怠Idle 於to 道way 路road,
不No 得obtain 操hold 事profession 者one,
七Seven 十ten 萬ten thousand 家family.

相Examine 守guard 數count 年year,
以By means of 爭conflict 一one 日day之's 勝victory,
而And yet 愛love 爵feudal 祿official salary 百hundred 金dollars,
不No 知know 敵enemy之's 情condition 者one,
不No 仁benevolence之's 至stop 也also.

非Weak 人men之's 將general 也also,
非Weak 主ruler之's 佐assistance 也also,
非Weak 勝victory之's 主master 也also.

Using Spies

Sun Tzu said:

Altogether, building an army requires thousands of men.
They invade and march thousands of miles.
Whole families are destroyed.
Other families must be heavily taxed.
Every day, thousands of dollars must be spent.

Internal and external events force people to move.
They are unable to work while on the road.
They are unable to find and hold a useful job.
This affects seventy percent of thousands of families.

You can watch and guard for years.
Then a single battle can determine victory in a day.
Despite this, bureaucrats hold onto their salary money too dearly.
They remain ignorant of the enemy's condition.
The result is cruel.

They are not leaders of men.
They are not servants of the state.
They are not masters of victory.

故Make 明bright 君monarch 賢worthy 將general,
所Place 以by means of 動movement 而and yet 勝win
人men,
成Accomplish 功attack 出exit 於to 眾crowd 者one,
先First 知know 也also;
先First 知know 者one,
不No 可can 取obtain 於to 鬼demon 神soul,
不No 可can 象image 於to 事profession,
不No 可can 驗check 於to 度degree,
必Must 取obtain 於from 人men,
知Know 敵enemy 之's 情condition 者one 也also.

故Make 用use 間spies 有have 五five:
有Have 鄉countryside 間spies,
有Have 內inside 間spies,
有Have 反reverse 間spies,
有Have 死dead 間spies,
有Have 生birth 間spies.

五Five 間spies 俱all 起rise,
莫Not 知know 其this 道philosophy,
是Correct 謂meaning 神spirit 紀arrange,
人Men 君monarch 之's 寶treasure 也also.

鄉Countryside 間spies 者one,
因Source 其this 鄉countryside 人men 而and yet 用use 之it.

內Inside 間spies 者one,
因Source 其this 官official 人men 而and yet 用use 之it.

反Reverse 間spies 者one,
因Source 其this 敵enemy 間spies 而and yet 用use 之it.

You need a creative leader and a worthy commander.
You must move your troops to the right places to beat others.
You must accomplish your attack and escape unharmed.
This requires foreknowledge.
You can obtain foreknowledge.
You can't get it from demons or spirits.
You can't see it from professional experience.
You can't check it with analysis.
You can only get it from other people.
You must always know the enemy's situation.

You must use five types of spies.
You need local spies.
You need inside spies.
You need double agents.
You need doomed spies.
You need surviving spies.

You need all five types of spies.
No one must discover your methods.
You will be then able to put together a true picture.
This is the commander's most valuable resource.

You need local spies.
Get them by hiring people from the countryside.

You need inside spies.
Win them by subverting government officials.

You need double agents.
Discover enemy agents and convert them.

死Dead 間spies 者one,
為Become 誑deluded 事profession 於to 外outside,
令Command 吾our 間spies 知know 之it,
而And yet 傳pass 於to 敵enemy.

生Birth 間spies 者one,
反Return 報report 也also.

☯

故 Make 三three 軍army之's 事job,
親Intimate 莫not 親intimate 於with 間spies,
賞Money 莫not 厚generous 於to 間spies,
事Profession 莫not 密secret 於to 間spies.

非Weak 聖sage 智wisdom 不no 能can 用use 間spies,
非Weak 仁love 義justice 不no 能can 使use 間spies,
非Weak 微tiny 妙subtle 不no 能can 得obtain 間spies 之of
實fullness.

微Tiny 哉alas! 微Trifling 哉alas!
無Without 所place 不no 能can 用use 間spies 也also.

間Spies 事profession 未do not 發distribute 而and yet 先first
聞hear 者things,
間Spies 與give 所place 告tell 者things 兼currently 皆together
死dead.

☯

136

You need doomed spies.
Deceive professionals into being captured.
We let them know our orders.
They then take those orders to our enemy.

You need surviving spies.
Someone must return with a report.

Your job is to build a complete army.
No relations are as intimate as they are with spies.
No rewards are too generous for spies.
No work is as secret as that of spies.

If you aren't clever and wise, you can't use spies.
If you aren't fair and just, you can't use spies.
If you can't see the small subtleties, you won't get the truth
from spies.

Pay attention to small, trifling details!
Spies are helpful in every area.

Spies are the first to hear information, so they must not
spread it.
Spies who give your location or talk to others must be killed
along with those to whom they have talked.

凡All 軍army 之's 所place 欲desire 擊strike,
城City wall 之's 所place 欲desire 攻attack,
人Men 之's 所place 欲desire 殺kill,
必Must 先first 知know 其this 守guard 將general,
左Left 右right,
謁Meet with superior 者one,
門Door 者one,
舍Huts 人men 之's 姓clan 名name,
令Command 吾our 間spies 必must 索demand 知know 之it.

必Must 知know 敵enemy 間spies 之of 來next 間spies 我my 者person,
因Source 而and yet 利benefit 之it,
導Lead 而and yet 舍shelter 之it,
故Make 反reverse 間spies 可can 得obtain 而and yet 用use 使envoy 也also.

因Source 是correct 而and yet 知know 之it,
故Make 鄉countryside 間spies, 內inside 間spies 可can 得obtain 而and yet 使use 也also;
因Source 是correct 而and yet 知know 之it,
故Make 死dead 間spies 為be 誑deluded 事profession,
可Can 使use 告tell 敵enemy;
因Source 是correct 而and yet 知know 之it,
故Make 生birth 間spies 可can 使use 如comparable to 期phase.

You may want to attack an army's position.
You may want to attack a certain fortification.
You may want to kill people in a certain place.
You must first know the guarding general.
You must know his left and right flanks.
You must know his hierarchy.
You must know the way in.
You must know where different people are stationed.
We must demand this information from our spies.

I want to know the enemy spies in order to convert new
spies into my men.
You find a source of information and bribe them.
You must bring them in with you.
You must obtain them as double agents and use them as your
emissaries.

Do this correctly and carefully.
You can contact both local and inside spies and obtain their
support.
Do this correctly and carefully.
You create doomed spies by deceiving professionals.
You can use them to give false information.
Do this correctly and carefully.
You must have surviving spies capable of bringing you
information at the right time.

五Five 間spies之's 事profession,
主Master 必must 知know 之it,
知Know 之it 必must 在exist 於from 反reverse 間spies,
故Make 反reverse 間spies 不no 可can 不not 厚generous
也also.

☯

昔Ancient 殷dance 之of 興prosperity 也also,
伊He 摯hold 在exist 夏dynasty.

周Cautious 之of 興prosperity 也also,
呂Spine 牙tooth 在exist 殷dance.

故Make 明bright 君monarch 賢worthy 將general,
能Can 以by mean of 上above 智wisdom 為become 間spy
者one,
必Must 成complete 大big 功achievement,
此Here 兵war之's 要need,
三Three 軍armies之's 所place 恃depend on 而and yet
動move 也also.

⦂⦂⦂

140

These are the five different types of intelligence work.
You must be certain to master them all.
You must be certain to create double agents.
You cannot afford to be too cheap in creating these double agents.

☯

This technique created the success of ancient emperors.
This is how they held their dynasties.

You must always be careful of your success.
Learn from the past examples.

Be a smart commander and good general.
You do this by using your best and brightest people for spying.
This is how you achieve the greatest success.
This is how you meet the necessities of war.
The whole army's position and ability to move depends on these spies.

❖❖❖

GLOSSARY OF CHINESE CHARACTERS
(Partial List)

能ability
上above
成accomplish
功accomplishment
積accumulate
行activity
附add to
進advance
利advantage
後afterwards
又again
獨alone
凡all
任allow
也also
雖although
中among
鎰amount of gold
銖amount of silver
昔ancient
古ancient
而and yet
怒anger
兵army
甲armor
至arrive
矢arrow
佐assist
進advance
攻attack
權authority
秋autumn
待await
旌banner
戰battle
故because

為become
起begin
下below
曲bend
大big
鳥bird
生birth
阻block
鈍blunt
廓boundless
勇bravery
旅brigade
明bright
破broken
于by
以by means of
謂call
可can
能can
虜capture
拙careless
帶carry
載carry
車cart
擒catch
變change
革change
篇chapter
輜chariot
擇choose
取choose
環circle
城city
姓clans
雷clap
聰clever
陰cloud
弊collapse

寒cold
色color
令command
如comparable to
全complete
爭conflict
蔽conceal
爭conflict
惑confused
屈consume
制control
治control
是correct
政correctness
安console
數count
算counts
過cross
弩crossbow
眾crowd
鍾cup (measure of volume)
伐cutdown
危danger
險dangerous
日day
晝daytime
死death
亡death
詭deceive
負defeat
銳defeat
敗defeat
守defend
保defend
索demand

離depart
欲desire
迂detour
直direct
方direction
害disadvantage
災disaster
難disaster
捐discard
罷dismiss
亂disorder
遠distant
距distance
分divide
動do
勿do not
疑doubtful
御drive
鼓drum
暮dusk
務duties
彼each other
耳ear
易easy
卵egg
丘empty
虛empty
終end
闔enclose
前enemy
誘entice
殫entirely
委entrust
當equal
器equipment
避evade
每every
察examine

餘 excess
忒 excess
盡 exhaust
在 exist
出 exit
勞 exert
經 experience
貴 expensive
通 expert
外 external
目 eye
向 face
後 fall behind
名 fame
姓 family
叵 fathom
畏 fear
心 feeling
寡 few
鬥 fight
火 fire
堅 firm
先 first
五 five
修 fix
旗 flag
漂 float
激 flow
從 follow
食 food
九 force
迫 force
形 form
原 former
林 forest
四 four
於 from
由 from
將 general
得 get
與 give

饋 give
予 give
膠 glue
去 go
善 good
谿 gorge
政 govern
司 government office
糧 grain
稈 grain
餘 great
地 ground
賓 guest
導 guide
和 harmoniously
有 has
半 half
未 have not
鸑 hawk
其 hay
聞 hear
輴 hearse
天 heaven
冑 helmet
周 help
此 here
豫 hesitate
衢 highway
暑 hot
馬 horse
鄉 hometown
駟 horse team
家 house
趨 hurry
夫 husband
加 increase
蟻 insect
親 intimate
意 intention
智 intelligence

內 internal
侵 invade
之 it
殺 kill
惰 lazy
佚 leisure
窮 limit
機 machine
故 make
處 manage
聚 masses
度 measure
交 meet
人 men
金 metal
法 methods
里 mile (measure of distance)
役 military service
雜 mixed
貨 money
月 month
朝 morning
陵 mound
山 mountain
渾 muddy
乘 multiply by
沌 murky
必 must
相 mutually
萬 myriad
名 name
狹 narrow
國 nation
性 nature
近 near
夜 night
不 no
侯 noblemen
陰 north, shady hillside

莫 not
未 not yet
數 number
觀 observe
撓 obstruct
險 obstruction
得 obtain
之 of
士 officer
一 one
逆 oppose
破 order
牛 ox
過 pass
傳 pass
頓 pause
安 peace
罰 penalize
民 people
人 people
任 permission
道 philosophy
地 place
所 place
計 plan, planning
掠 plunder
澤 pond
措 position
貧 poverty, poor
窮 poor
勢 power
力 power
強 powerful
備 prepare
保 preserve
患 problem
循 proceed
事 profession
沮 prevention
驕 proud
貧 poverty

養provide for
糧provisions
公public
引pull
拔pull out
量quantity
急quickly
怒rage
及reach
舉raise
奉receive
受receive
籍record
恃rely on
節restrain
歸return home
復return to
賞reward
江river
途roadway
轉roll
圓round
櫓row
圮ruined
治rule
主ruler
同same
飽satisfaction
藏save
曰say
寡scarce
謀scheme
校school
時season
次second-rate
見see
若seem
睹seen
奪seize
己self
自self

賣sell
分separate
侍serve
七seven
挫sharp
舍shelter
盾shield
發shoot
示show
同similar
情situation
況situation
六six
事skill
巧skillful
味smell
然so
卒soldier
因source
陽south, sunny hillside
言speak
速speed
馳speed
氣spirit
隙split
始start
飢starving
主state
石stone
已stop
至stop
止stop
正straight
謀strategy
行step
河stream
嚴strict
求strive for
強strong
修study

實substantial
足sufficient
食supplies
屈surrender
懸suspend
疾swift
戟sword
制system
取take
紜tangled
示teach
術technique
廟temple
十ten
萬ten thousand
嘗taste
孰that
則then
乃therefore
者thing
此this
其this
千thousand
毫thousandth
三three
於through
投throw
駑thrown down
霆thunder
縻tie up
乘times
倍times
聲tone
嚮towards
練train
靜tranquil
木tree
師troops
信trust
廿twenty
謂understanding

伍unit
兼unite
奇unusual
譁uproar
使use
用use, useful
彈use up
諸various
勝victory
見view
暴violent
客visitor
邱walls
兵war
決wash
曹waste
輜wagon
闕watchtower
水water
吾we
非weak
財wealth
勞weary
天weather
稱weigh
廣wide
矣will be
勝win
風wind
智wisdom
孰which
退withdrawn
無without
虞worry

Amazing Secrets!

Amazing Secrets of Sun Tzu's The Art of War unveils all the hidden secrets of the famous treatise on competition. For the first time, you can see graphically the complex relationships that Sun Tzu teaches in his text. Only in this book will you discover all the hidden symbols and metaphors Sun Tzu used to describe his system of competition.

Like our other books, you get two books side-by-side. You get our complete translation of *The Art of War.* On the facing page, you get a complete explanation in words and pictures of Sun Tzu's method of competition.

Amazing Secrets of Sun Tzu's The Art of War gives tools you need to apply Sun Tzu's system to any form of strategic competition. It would take you years of study to uncover even a fraction of the secrets offered here and nowhere else. Gary Gagliardi, America's leading authority on using Sun Tzu's system in business, developed this powerful method of teaching Sun Tzu's system.

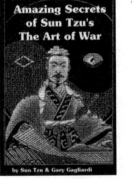

Amazing Secrets of Sun Tzu's The Art of War
ISBN: 1929194072
Paperback. $14.95.
Available: June, 2001

Clearbridge Publishing books may be purchased for business, for any promotional use, or for special sales. Please contact:

Clearbridge Publishing
Phone: (206) 533-9357
Fax: (206) 546-9756
P.O. Box 33772, Shoreline, WA 98133
E-mail: info@clearbridge.com.
Web: www.clearbridge.com

For Sales Professionals

The Art of War & The Art of Sales takes Sun Tzu's lessons and shows you how to specifically apply them to today's problems of contacting customers, convincing them to buy, and winning their on-going business. If you are responsible for sales or sales management, you will want this version of *The Art of War* written to address the needs of individual sales people fighting for orders from buyers. If you manage a sales force, you will want to buy this version of Sun Tzu for your people to study.

Like *The Art of War & The Art of Management*, you get two books side-by-side. You get our translation of *The Art of War*. Additionally, you get Sun Tzu's ideas interpreted line-by-line to help working sales professionals in the battle for sales. If you are a sales manager or company president, you will be more than happy with the results of your sales people following Sun Tzu's advice. This is a book they will read and a philosophy they will use. The enemy is the competition. The battleground is the customer's mind. Victory is winning an on-going relationship with the customer. The two versions are shown side-by-side to give you a complete picture of using Sun Tzu's approach to modern selling.

The Art of War & The Art of Sales
ISBN: 1929194013
Paperback. $14.95.

Clearbridge Publishing books may be purchased for business, for any promotional use, or for special sales. Please contact:

Clearbridge Publishing
Phone: (206) 533-9357
Fax: (206) 546-9756
P.O. Box 33772, Shoreline, WA 98133
E-mail: info@clearbridge.com.
Web: www.clearbridge.com

Winning Markets

The Art of War & The Art of Marketing takes Sun Tzu's lessons and helps you use them to identify markets, position against the competition, and win battles in the marketplace. You can almost directly apply the lessons of *The Art of War* to the marketing of your company and its products. *The Art of Marketing* gives you Sun Tzu's ideas in a form that addresses the strategic issues of competition in today's terminology.

Like *The Art of War & The Art of Management*, you get both books side-by-side. You get our translation of *The Art of War*. Additionally, you get Sun Tzu's ideas interpreted line-by-line to help you win the real-world battles in the marketplace.

The Art of War & The Art of Marketing deals with the external issues of winning customer awareness and generating sales. In many ways, it is the perfect companion book to *The Art of Management,* the book you currently hold in your hand, which focuses on the internal organization. Using them together, you can address both the internal and external concerns of your organization.

The Art of War & The Art of Marketing
ISBN: 1929194021
Paperback. $14.95.

Clearbridge Publishing books may be purchased for business, for any promotional use, or for special sales. Please contact:

Clearbridge Publishing
Phone: (206) 533-9357
Fax: (206) 546-9756
P.O. Box 33772, Shoreline, WA 98133
E-mail: info@clearbridge.com.
Web: www.clearbridge.com

Managing Organizations

The Art of War & The Art of Management applies Sun Tzu's techniques to building a competitve organization. A companion work to our externally-focused sales and marketing versions, this book addresses the internal issues of competition: motivating your people and continuous improvement of your processes and products. It apples the competitive techniques of Sun Tzu to creating an externally focused organization.

Like *The Art of War & The Art of Sales*, you get both books side-by-side. You get our translation of *The Art of War.* You also get Sun Tzu's ideas interpreted line-by-line to help you deal with the typical problems that all managers must address.

The Art of War & The Art of Management deals with the internal issues of attracting good people, training them, and teaching them to understand the business of competition. It also teaches managers to rethink their business processes from the viewpoint of a competitive marketplace. It is the perfect campanion book for those who want to get their internal functions in line with the external sales and marketing focus of their company.

The Art of War & The Art of Management
ISBN: 1929194056
Paperback. $14.95.

Clearbridge Publishing books may be purchased for business, for any promotional use, or for special sales. Please contact:

Clearbridge Publishing
Phone: (206) 533-9357
Fax: (206) 546-9756
Mail: P.O. Box 33772, Shoreline, WA 98133
E-mail: info@clearbridge.com.
Web: www.clearbridge.com